EASTCOTE
From Village to Suburb

*A Short Social History
1900 – 1945*

by

Ron Edwards

HILLINGDON BOROUGH LIBRARIES
1987

© London Borough of Hillingdon 1987

ISBN 0-907869-09-2
Cover illustration – "Eastcote by
District Railway" by Chas Pears,
courtesy of the London Transport Museum.
Printed by Echo Press (1983) Ltd.,
Loughborough and London.

CONTENTS

List of Illustrations   5

Introduction   7

CHAPTER 1.   EASTCOTE AT THE BEGINNING OF THE 20TH CENTURY   9
Geography and physical appearance – large houses and small homes – farms – diseases – poverty – Institute – local welfare and entertainments – schools – menus.

CHAPTER 2.   FIRST STEPS IN CHANGE   21
Metropolitan Railway link to Uxbridge – new developments – sewers and main water – visitors – new Urban District Council – reports on state of housing – Town Plan 1914 – British Freeholds Investments Syndicate – individual plans – lack of working class housing – Ruislip Manor Cottage Society.

CHAPTER 3.   "LONDON'S LATEST IDEAL AND PICTURESQUE RESIDENTIAL SUBURB"   31
Post 1918 – council housing – Telling Brothers – change of centre – 1930s speculative building – package deals – expansion of shopping facilities – new building south of railway – and north of village – travelling difficulties.

CHAPTER 4.   CHURCHES, CLUBS AND OTHER SOCIAL CENTRES   51
Social demands from early newcomers – new types of resident – start of Womens Institute – St Lawrence Church – St Thomas More – St Andrews URC – Methodists – tennis and bowls clubs – recreation ground – new schools – children's activities.

CHAPTER 5.   EASTCOTE IN WARTIME   61
First World War – voluntary hospital – casualties – new Health Visitor – September 1939 – preparing for air raids – effects of blackout – shelters – travel – food supplies – Northolt aerodrome – operations room – effect of raids – wartime industries – Eastcote Place.

CHAPTER 6.   POSTSCRIPT   73

Acknowledgements and Sources   75

Index   76

ILLUSTRATIONS

	Page
Eastcote Village 1897	8
Dean Cottage and The Rosery, Eastcote Village circa 1920	10
Eastcote Smithy, mid 1930s	12
Fore Street Farm just prior to demolition	13
Eastcote House just prior to demolition	14
Haydon Hall in its later years	16
Advertisement of the 1920s	18
Houses in Bridle Road built 1912	25
Houses in Cheney Street built 1912-13	26
25/27 Fore Street, built by Ruislip Manor Cottage Society in 1914	28
Eastcote End Park Estate, advertisement from "Metro-Land" 1924	30
Eastcote Station looking towards Uxbridge, mid 1930's	33
Morford Way, built by Telling Bros 1924	35
Plan of Rotherham Estates' Deane Estate	36
Hawthorne Avenue 1930	38
Petition for better roads 1930	39
Meadow Way, a Rotherham Estates development	40
The author's first house in Eastcote, Deane Croft Road, 1932	41
Deane Croft Road, 1986	41
Field End Road, shopping centre at time of Silver Jubilee 1935	43
Eastcote Park Estate, October 1933	45
Deane Parade, Field End Road	47
Projected plans for Eastcote Station 1937	48
Eastcote Station c. 1947	49
St. Lawrence's church at time of construction, October 1933	56
War Memorial	60
1940 Air Raid Incident Map	63
Decontamination Centre remaining in Haydon Hall grounds	66
How Eastcote village had begun to expand by 1935	72

INTRODUCTION

It is now 23 years since Mr W. A. G. Kemp published his history of Eastcote, a testimony to his affection for the district, which drew on many sources, including the memories of longtime residents, to give others an insight into the older village community. Since that time, his book has given much pleasure to thousands of readers and led to the formation of groups who have continued his work. Without doubt, this movement has helped to create an interest in, and enhancement of, the many delightful aspects of the present locality.

The writer of this present work was also inspired by the enthusiasm of Mr Kemp, and having lived in Eastcote for over 55 years has witnessed many of the changes which transformed a rural community into a thriving and attractive suburb of Greater London. This volume aims to set out some of those steps of change and the effects which events had on the growing community. It is not an attempt to create a definitive work on that exciting era but hopefully it will help those who have only known Eastcote since the end of the Second World War to appreciate the scale of change and to understand the way of life, now long forgotten, which existed at the beginning of the century.

The present volume has been compiled from the personal recollections of the writer and other Eastcote residents and also from a variety of sources, official and personal, which have been made available. Grateful thanks are due to all who have assisted in any way.

Ron Edwards

Chapter One

Eastcote at the beginning of the 20th century

If we owned a 'time machine' and could return to the early years of this century we would find Eastcote to be a small community of some 600 people in around 120 houses. The majority of the population lived in scattered farms and cottages on the old road net-work, namely, Bridle Road, Catlins Lane, Cheney Street, Cuckoo Hill, Field End Road, Fore Street, High Road, Joel Street, Southill Lane and Wiltshire Lane. At this time Fore Street was locally called Frog Lane – said to be so named after a large pond almost opposite to Four Elms Farm – as was the southern end of Field End Road called Northolt Road and its western end where it approached the High Road, Chapel Hill.

In addition to these farms and cottages there were four large houses of varying ages, a few mid Victorian villas, a smithy, four beer houses or public houses and a Methodist chapel. There was no shopping centre, public transport, radio, television, telephones, gas or electricity. Mains water and a sewage system were only just beginning to percolate through the district.

The parish church was at Ruislip but if you had been of Catholic or other non-conformist religious persuasion you would have had to go to Harrow, Ickenham or Uxbridge. The nearest railway was at Pinner where the Metropolitan had opened a station in 1885 or at Hatch End where the London and North Western Railway main line from Euston to the Midlands and North operated. If, therefore, you did not possess your own carriage – and very few did – you either hired a horse cab from Mr Wright at Haydon Hall stables – and not many could afford this – or you walked to your destination. However, walking presented hazards as roads and pathways were often in an unmade condition. The Ruislip Parish Council, who were the immediate local authority, complained in the early months of 1900 to the Uxbridge Rural District Council, who were the Highway Authority, about the bad condition of the footways in Eastcote and Ruislip which, with few exceptions, had not been ballasted for over three years.

In 1907, Dr Hignett, Medical Officer of Health to the newly formed Ruislip-Northwood Urban District Council, described the area as having a mainly clay subsoil which retained surface water in wet weather until it was removed by evaporation. Surface water, either in shallow puddles or more severe flooding, would not have assisted travel by road in

Eastcote Village 1897.

Eastcote — From Village to Suburb

carriage or on foot and would have been a contributory cause to the bad condition of footways and roads. None of these factors encouraged regular travel, unless essential, during the period from October to March, particularly as Dr Hignett also comments on the atmosphere being damp with ground mists in autumn and winter.

Geographically, although not so obvious today, Eastcote reaches 312 feet above sea level at its northern extremity at Haste Hill and than gradually falls away to 120 feet above sea level around the area where the present 'Eastcote Arms' stands in the south. Running diagonally across the district is the River Pinn which has its sources on Harrow Weald Common and Pinner Hill and eventually flows into the River Colne at Yiewsley. These geographical features, together with the nature of the subsoil, had been of importance in determining the nature and layout of the earlier village. A quick reference to a map will show that the older community was centred around the River Pinn at about 140 feet above sea level. Although hard to work, the nature of the land made it very fertile although good management of drainage was necessary to overcome the surface water problem. As many contemporary gardeners are aware, dry weather can be as much a problem as wet weather when one has a clay subsoil.

These natural conditions, however, were also conducive to good growth of trees, shrubs and hedgerows as can be seen today in our

Dean Cottage and the Rosery, Eastcote Village circa 1920.

Eastcote at the beginning of the 20th century

present gardens, parkland and open spaces. Although there were no remnants of the old forest of Middlesex in the Eastcote area, hedgerows abounded as field boundaries, particularly those planted following the Parliamentary Enclosure Acts of the early 19th century. Nineteenth century roads in a rural area were normally about 25 feet wide with some variations for greens alongside trackways and roads. By the beginning of the 20th century roadside trees planted early in the previous century had grown to a good level of maturity and this, coupled with relatively narrow width, resulted in roads which, in summer had a near canopy of leafage but in autumn and winter were near impassable because of considerable leaf fall, with no district-wide organised street cleaning and reliance on ditches for drainage. Taking all of these factors into account, the wetness and possible surface flooding, unmaintained roads, shaded in summer but miserable in autumn, winter and early spring the district would have had a luxuriant appearance in summer, but would have seemed somewhat dripping and stark for the remainder of the year. The earlier part of this century also experienced somewhat more severe winters. We can, therefore, visualise a landscape which would have been full of attractions in summer with a wealth of flowering field and hedgerow plants from March onwards and with fruits in autumn but the winter conditions, lacking our 1980s street lighting, cleansing and paving, would have been far from inviting.

In spite of these conditions the Eastcote community continued to exist and multiply in the early 1900s. Who were they and what did they do? Examination of contemporary records presents a picture of two communities with limited interrelationship. On the one hand there was a minority who were reasonably or very affluent and on the other a majority who were poor or very poor. The former group were the owners and occupants of the four large houses – Eastcote House originating in the early 16th century, Haydon Hall probably with an origin in the 17th century, High Grove dating as a major house from the 18th century, but much rebuilt in the late 19th century and New House, later Eastcote Place, also built in the late 19th century. In 1900 John Boyle and his family were living at Eastcote House, although the house was still owned by Mr R. Hawtrey Deane of West Kensington, a descendant of the Hawtreys who built the house; Captain and Mrs Bennett Edwards were at Haydon Hall; Hugh, Alice and Eleanor Warrender were owners of High Grove but all of them were not in constant residence, and Captain Sullivan occupied New House. Captain Bennett Edwards had been one of the founders of the Northwood Golf Club in 1891 and Mrs Bennett Edwards was herself a wealthy woman whose father had been successful in the legal profession, leaving her and her brothers valuable publishing interests as well as real estate. She was a novelist and had been a pioneer in the 19th century movement for the emancipation of women. Hugh Warrender had a commission in the Grenadier Guards, Alice was founder of the Hawthornden Prize for Literature at Oxford and Eleanor was to

Eastcote — From Village to Suburb

Eastcote Smithy, mid 1930s.

distinguish herself nursing during wartime. Their brother, also joint owner, was Vice Admiral Sir George Warrender, 7th Baronet of Lochend from 1901. He had married Maud, the youngest daughter of the 8th Earl of Shaftesbury. Due to his involvement in Naval affairs from the age of 18 till his death in 1917 they spent much of their lives travelling abroad.

    The Warrenders were grandchildren of Sir Hugh Hume-Campbell's first marriage. Through his second marriage, to Juliana Rebecca Fuller, he acquired High Grove and also a useful relationship to the Prime Minister, Sir Robert Peel, his uncle by marriage. Sir Robert's son Arthur, later to become Speaker of the House of Commons and first Viscount Peel, was therefore a cousin by marriage. This family's many links by marriage to the peerage and particularly the close friendship with Lady Randolph Churchill, probably explain why the Dowager Queen of Sweden and Winston Churchill both stayed at High Grove in the early 1900s, she for a period of convalescence, he as part of his honeymoon.

    The majority of the population were not well off, in fact many were very poor. Most worked locally and were involved in agriculture which was the main occupation of the district. Some practised trades – blacksmith and farrier, coachbuilder, builder, wood dealer. Others worked in the households of the large houses or outside servicing them. There was a market gardener, David Crack at Field End, two publicans and two beer retailers. Henry Gallop doubled up as builder and

Eastcote at the beginning of the 20th century

sub-postmaster at the Old Barn House in the village. There was, however, an intermediate social group such as those who lived in the mid-19th century Field End Villas in Chapel Hill with middle class and professional backgrounds, Eastcote Lodge in the village (demolished 1963 and replaced by Flag Walk); Spring Cottage (now Flag Cottage) nearby where Miss Carter ran a private school; Eastcote Point at the top of Cuckoo Hill with The Circuits opposite, the latter more strictly in the Parish of Pinner, and farms which were gradually being converted into middle class residential properties. Among these were Hornend (then called 'Brooklands') in Cheney Street, Sigers in Field End Road with Field End House opposite (now the site of St Thomas More R C church), The Grange in the High Road, Southill Farm in Southill Lane and The Barns also in Field End Road. The latter is now demolished and replaced by Farthings Close, the only remnant being Retreat Cottage which has been partially converted from one of the range of barns.

A variety of small farms functioned around the village community, Cuckoo Hill Farm and Mistletoe Farm in Cuckoo Hill; Cheney Farm, Cheney Street; Joel Street Farm and Myrtle Farm on the east side of Joel Street beyond the 'Ship'; Haydon Hall Farm standing on the corner of Joel Street and Wiltshire Lane (where Ascott Court now stands); Ivy Farm in Wiltshire Lane; Fore Street Farm and Four Elms Farm in Fore Street; Field End Farm in Field End Road opposite the War Memorial; New Model Farm, Northolt Road and in the south of the district Bourne Farm which stood at the junction of Long Drive and The

Fore Street Farm just prior to demolition.

Eastcote — From Village to Suburb

Eastcote House just prior to demolition.

Fairway until its recent demolition. In earlier centuries north Middlesex had been a mainly arable farming area but following the repeal of the Corn Laws in 1846 and the imports of wheat from North America later in the 19th century, it became more profitable to change over to hay growing. The growing London market was close at hand with its increasing demand for fodder for horse transport. Some arable farming continued and small numbers of cattle, milk cows and pigs were raised. An indication of how small the proportion of these latter was is shown by the fact that the whole area of Ruislip, Northwood and Eastcote only had about 200 milk cows and imported milk during the early 1900s to satisfy a total population of around 6000.

The quality and management of milk production at this time did not altogether satisfy the standards expected by the Medical Officer of Health. In 1908 he noted that although all but three of the 27 cowkeepers and dairymen on the Council register had mains water supply laid on, most of the cowsheds were old and badly constructed and could not be converted into modern, well paved, ventilated and drained habitation for cows. Even in 1913 he mentions that four of the cowsheds were converted old barns so faulty in construction that they could never be improved to modern standards. He was inclined to blame the landlords for this state of

Eastcote at the beginning of the 20th century

affairs rather than the occupiers. In 1908 no systematic tuberculin testing was carried out and the MoH recommended twice yearly testing with better hygiene at milking places. The TT procedure was speedily brought into being and the number of cows affected was found to be small.

The MoH's reports are of great value in attempting to assess the standard of living at the beginning of the century, because one sees the conflict emerging between the older conservative way of life and work and the new ideas arising from scientific and medical research. For example, he made the following statements in 1913: *"A supply of pure clean milk is absolutely essential to the health of the community. Milk that is not kept clean is one of the chief agents in producing fatal diarrhoea in young children." "Tubercular disease in children is largely produced by tuberculous milk."*

Both pulmonary and non pulmonary TB were rife during this period. They could affect all social classes, and death from TB was so often the end of heroines in opera. Only a little imagination is required to visualise how much greater the incidence was among under nourished children and young people of the poorer classes. Living conditions for many were reflected in two comments in the MoH's report in 1911 concerning Ruislip and Eastcote specifically: *"Most of the cottages are very old and in a generally dilapidated condition, yet there is a great demand for these cottages, poor as they are, there being seldom one empty." "At Ruislip and Eastcote there are a number of cottages of such ancient date and in such a bad state of repair that it seems impossible to put them into a thoroughly sanitary condition without reconstructing them entirely."* He was concerned in 1913 that in some dwellings ceilings were as low as 6'2" and floors were below ground level. Many cottages were very old, badly lighted and badly ventilated.

As well as the dangers of TB and diarrhoea in young children there was very real exposure to other diseases which have largely disappeared today. Whooping cough, scarlet fever and diptheria could be rampant. In May 1906 the Infants School at Ruislip had 35 out of 55 absent with whooping cough. In 1909 there were 27 notified cases of scarlet fever at Ruislip Schools in the summer and autumn terms and when measles and German measles were added to the Notifiable List in 1916, 61 cases were reported in that year, 202 in 1917 at the Ruislip and Northwood Schools and 232 in 1918. This gives some indication of the risks that children in the area ran. It becomes more poignant when an examination of the mortality statistics shows that, except in two years, between 1906 and 1915 the proportion of total deaths occurring to children under the age of one ranged from 10.8% to 21.3%. In the same years the proportion of deaths occurring under the age of 15 ranged from 21.7% to 38.2%. These figures should be compared with 2.6% under the age of 1 in 1970, and 3.5% under 15 in the same year.

15

Poverty can be illustrated by reference to other events. In the Parish magazine of St Martin's, Ruislip in April 1901 it was reported that distribution of Jeremiah Bright's Charity of Bread and Beef (founded 1721) had been made to 25 poor families of Eastcote on Xmas Eve 1900, and that Lady Hume Campbell's Charity of Coal had been distributed in February 1901 to 40 families in Eastcote. This last named had, with additional contributions, enabled 5 cwt to be given to each family. Based on our earlier estimate of about 120 houses in Eastcote at this time, if we exclude 25 as those belonging to wealthy and middle class families we find over 25% of Eastcote households qualifying for Bright's Charity and over 40% for Lady Campbell's. These figures are not out of line with those published by Seebohm Rowntree in 1901 based on his social survey made in York which suggested that nearly 30% of the total population existed below the poverty line. Rural areas could be in the worst of positions, particularly in the South of England, as their produce was very dependent on weather conditions and the only competition for labour was in London which also attracted immigrants from other surrounding country areas as well as from Europe. There was fairly constant movement of population seeking better opportunities for work. The towns offered the greater range of opportunities for both girls and boys, as the former's main employment opportunities were to be found in domestic service and there were many households in growing London looking for cheap domestic servants.

The picture painted so far of Eastcote at the beginning of the 20th century is somewhat gloomy, but is more realistic than the image of

Haydon Hall in its later years.

the 'golden' countryside where every cottage had roses and honeysuckle round its door. Where roses and honeysuckle grew, they usually covered a high degree of deficiency in the basic household amenities required for a comfortable standard of living in an age when there was no Welfare State only self help or distributions from local charities. It is at this point that we see a social relationship between the various groups who made up the total community, as not only did the more affluent provide work for some but they also contributed towards various aspects of the welfare of the less fortunate. Life styles for those living in small rural communities at the beginning of the 20th century, reflected status, employment and level of income. Affluence meant a comfortable life with a variety of household goods and food and employment of domestic servants.

As one went down the income scale so these facilities diminished until they almost disappeared. For many in employment, the hours were long and the work arduous. Such niceties as job satisfaction and working conditions were much dependent on the employer and his or her attitude towards employees and the ability of the employee to adapt to conditions. It has been argued by many that although rural poverty was equal to or worse than that in urban areas, the rural dweller always had the advantage of living in the fresh air surrounded by nature which could be most enchanting when the sun was shining even if uncomfortable during wet miserable weather. A very good idea of how a country child saw this can be obtained from Flora Thompson's description of her childhood in 'Larkrise to Candleford'.

An insight into the support given to the poorer classes of the neighbourhood by their more affluent neighbours can be seen by looking at the record of contributors to local social events and clubs as recorded in the Ruislip Parish Magazine for the opening years of the century. The Ruislip National Schools in Eastcote Road to which a proportion of Eastcote children went, was supported in part by voluntary subscribers; the Eastcote Institute, a social club mainly for men, opened in 1893, was assisted by money contributions, magazines, books and papers from wealthier residents who also contributed services at entertainments given mainly for working people and their families and friends. The Institute building stood at this time in the small meadow in the High Road opposite to Eastcote Lodge. One of the main supporters was L. Ingham Baker who was the Vicar of Ruislip's brother in law and lived at Eastcote Lodge until 1900. An Eastcote Mother's Outing was organised by Mrs Abercrombie of Southill and went to the Earls Court Exhibition in 1900 and 1901. Mr Abercrombie, also an Overseer of the Poor, was Treasurer of the Eastcote Slate Club as well as being a financial supporter of Ruislip Schools and other functions. An Old Persons Tea (over 55!) was given at the Ruislip Schools and to sustain physical needs Coal, Clothing and Shoe Clubs were run for the parish needy. People who would be entitled to

17

Eastcote — From Village to Suburb

The Ship Inn,
EASTCOTE,
Charmingly Situated near PINNER.

1¼ Miles (across the Fields) from METROPOLITAN RAILWAY STATION.

TEAS.
Bread and Butter, One New Laid Egg and Preserve 0 1 0

LUNCHEONS.
Cut from the Joint with Two Vegetables, Pastry, Bread and Cheese 0 1 9

Plate of Cold Meat, Bread, Cheese and Pickles 0 1 0

SEDGWICK'S ALES, STOUT & BOTTLED BEERS.
SUPERIOR WINES, SPIRITS AND CIGARS.

Advertisement of the 1920s.

Eastcote at the beginning of the 20th century

receive goods from these clubs contributed their pence and the gentry contributed pounds.

Two major supporters of these community efforts were Mr and Miss Warrender of High Grove and Mrs Bennett Edwards of Haydon Hall. Not only were the former financial supporters of all types of social activity but Hugh Warrender was also a Manager of the Ruislip Schools, and Miss Warrender entertained occupants of the Church Houses of Ruislip at tea parties in High Grove. Similarly, Mrs Bennett Edwards was a financial contributor and in addition gave an annual party for children from Ruislip, Northwood and Pinner Schools in the grounds of Haydon Hall. According to the August 1901 Parish magazine the party in that year numbered 600 and entertainments included a roundabout, swings, a rifle gallery, donkeys to ride, games, races and a sumptuous tea. It is interesting to note that the invitation was limited to girls under 14 and boys under 12. Either this reflects a disparity in distribution of the sexes or Mrs Bennett Edwards was practical in assessing the potentiality for mischief between the two sexes.

The schools available to children were the National Schools in Eastcote Road, Ruislip and in School Lane, Pinner. The Council School in Pinner Road, Northwood which was attended by a proportion of children from Eastcote of a later generation, was not opened until 1910. Private schools were not plentiful and where they existed catered for the children from more affluent backgrounds. Miss Carter ran the small private school at Spring Cottage, but otherwise private schools could be found at Northwood, Harrow, Ealing, Watford, Pinner or Uxbridge.

As mentioned earlier, life style at home was directly related to means. The larger and middle class households would aim towards the more elaborate levels of eating as advocated by Mrs Beeton and High Grove could afford to have a housekeeper working and organising the household from 6.30 am to 11 pm. As well as large houses having a team of servants with specialist jobs, visitors would bring their own personal servants and London caterers would be brought in for particular occasions. The large houses also employed outdoor servants for transport and for maintenance of buildings and grounds. High Grove employed 6 gardeners before 1914, and the status of the head gardener at Haydon Hall is reflected by his accommodation – the present Haydon Lodge. These examples may be contrasted with the means available for the majority of villagers when in 1913 the MoH in considering the availability of houses for the working classes suggested that 6/- (30p) a week would be a reasonable level of rental to pay.

Storage for foodstuffs for all would be considered inadequate by present day housekeepers but was of the greatest difficulty for the working classes. Diet was, for them, rather basic; meat less common than cereal or vegetable. Meals aimed to be few and filling without elaborations. Recipes being printed as 'Homely Cookery' in 1901 included Toad-in-the-Hole, Hotch-Potch, Potato Pudding, Barley Soup, Boiled Eels, Baked Beefsteak Pudding, Cornflour Pudding, Raisin Pudding, Baked Rice Pudding, Toast and Water, Mutton Hodge-Podge, Vegetable Pie, Suffolk Dumplings, Tapioca Soup, Bread Pudding, Pea Soup, Seed Cake and Plum Pudding.

Chapter Two
First steps in change

On Thursday, June 30th, 1904 a rather fine lunch was served at Uxbridge during the official opening ceremony of the Harrow to Uxbridge Railway, which was part of the growing Metropolitan Railway system. The event was fully reported in the Middlesex & Buckinghamshire Advertiser of July 2nd. Reading that report, one or two observations made by reporter and official speakers strike the eye. For example, a report of the journey by the official train from Harrow to Uxbridge contained the following: *"...indeed the country between Harrow and Uxbridge is beautiful in the extreme. On Thursday, bathed in glorious sunshine, and scented with new mown hay, the countryside was at its best. Here stretches of meadowland, with herds of sleek cattle grazing lazily, there the clink and rattle of the grass cutting machines. Again, to mark as it were, the rural aspect of the new line, plump partridges raised their startled heads and a pheasant, with its glorious plumage shining like burnished gold ran to cover. And all this almost within the sound of Bow Bells!"*

A lyrical description but the same report makes mention of the Chairman of the Metropolitan Railway saying during the course of his speech that *"the making of the railway would open up a new district. That was carrying out the policy of the late chairman, Sir Edward Watkins, who always urged that the only salvation for a railway like the Metropolitan was to push out its borders further to the north. Their only chance was a suburban traffic." "Wherever he put down a line and erected a station, there buildings were erected.... It would not be done in a day.... But time was on their side. They had a beautiful country to open up...."* The same report quotes another speech by Mr A. Bailey, chairman of the Uxbridge Rural District Council, who produced laughter when he said that although he had been born in Uxbridge, he had never in his whole life been to Harrow! Sir Christopher Furness MP, a director of the Metropolitan, urged the owners of property to facilitate the development of the district, *"and speaking as a director of the Metropolitan Railway, which had found the necessary money to build the line to Uxbridge, he thought the directors had a right to ask those who lived in that interesting district to do their part to see that the capital outlay should not become a burden on the other parts of the line..."*

This blending of rural delights, subtle commercialism and parochial personal views may seem somewhat bizarre in the 1980s. Nevertheless, one must see all of these remarks in the context of the times. Victoria had died only three and a half years previously. Early

Eastcote — From Village to Suburb

Edwardian Britain was continuing the political and commercial philosophies which had grown out of the great progress in industrialisation and communication made during her reign; a period which had also seen a nation of rural communities change to one which was mainly urban. New opportunities for work had developed and in particular the growing middle classes were continually reaching out for improvements in personal standards of living particularly as expressed in ownership of an extending range of consumer goods and utilities.

When the new railway opened, the only intermediate station between Harrow and Uxbridge was at Ruislip and two years were to pass before a halt was created at Eastcote. As we have seen in the preceding chapter some new middle class development had occurred during the 19th century with the building of the semi-detached villas in Chapel Hill. These represented the earliest speculative development in Eastcote to be aimed at a specific social class. Northwood – its Metropolitan station opening in 1887 – was witnessing Francis Murray Maxwell Hallowell Carew's exploitation of the Eastbury Estate. Development had occurred at Greenhill following the opening of the Metropolitan Railway Station at Harrow in 1880. More would come at Ruislip as Kings College, lord of the manor and main landowner, realised the greater potential of building as investment on their lands compared with the lower returns being obtained from agriculture at that time.

By 1905 an 8″ main sewer ran from Cuckoo Hill to the Eastcote Pumping Station which was sited on the North side of Eastcote Road just past Fore Street. This had feeders into Cheney Street, Catlins Lane, Wiltshire Lane, Field End and Chapel Hill. Mains water from the Colne Valley Water Company was becoming available in the same area. Regular refuse collection under contract was in operation in the Ruislip, Northwood and Eastcote areas serving 36.8% of houses in 1906 and increasing up to 77% by 1915. Transport, sewage, refuse disposal and mains water supply, therefore, gradually became available in Eastcote between the beginning of the 20th century and the outbreak of war in 1914. The pleasures of the attractive countryside had been sampled by many thousands who had visited the district by cycle or other forms of transport on weekend and holiday outings during the summer months. Tea gardens catered for this trade in the village at the 'Rosery'; between the Old Barn and Eastcote Cottage and at the 'Ship' in Joel Street. All was ready for the development anticipated and hoped for by the Metropolitan Railway. Initially, however, development was slow, but building was taking place at Ruislip following the opening of the railway, and Northwood continued to expand.

At this point it would be well to stop and look at the changes which were occurring in local civic administration as this would effect the future development of the three areas of Ruislip, Northwood and Eastcote. The changes which took place throughout Britain during the

First steps in change

19th century were felt everywhere, and although the local districts remained basically rural up to the beginning of the 20th century it is clear that new thinking was emerging within the more affluent families. The 19th century saw an increase in the middle classes whose incomes were derived from new commercial and administrative occupations, as well as financial investment and the professions. During the same period the level of incomes for the working classes did not increase at the same rate, unless younger people broke away from traditional working backgrounds to enter the new skilled trades which had become available. The gap between rich and poor widened and those unable to follow the doctrine of 'self-help' which had been preached from the 1850s were becoming more disadvantaged requiring the social supports mentioned in the previous chapter. London's boundaries were getting closer annually, and industry was commencing at Wealdstone and Hayes.

In this changing society new social demands were emerging. The desire of the new middle classes to live in modern purpose built accommodation with up to date facilities was, to some extent, catered for by a growing army of builders whose scale of operations was increasing. Many of them were without experience of speculative building but the incentive to make money and obtain a good return on capital investment was there and was encouraged by the ethos of the times. A variety of Parliamentary Acts had been passed to cope with civil and public health problems but many of them were of an enabling character rather than compulsory. Local people felt the strains of the times and moves were made, albeit slowly, to deal with these new situations. In 1894 the Local Government Act had transferred some powers of local civil administration from the Vestry to a new Ruislip Parish Council with elected members from the three districts, but responsibility for highways and public utilities was with the Uxbridge Rural District Council. When it came to the provision of adequate drainage, strains between the older and newer communities became apparent. A conflict arose between the more conservative approach which continually looked at the cost of new innovations and the clamour from the new middle class residents of Northwood who were aware of the deficiencies in drainage and were not prepared to tolerate cesspools and the dangers of such diseases as diptheria and scarlet fever. As early as 1894 residents of Northwood had wanted Urban Council powers, and almost annually thereafter there were complaints as to the effectiveness of the Uxbridge Rural District Council in meeting the growing demands of the inhabitants of the Ruislip Parish. Attempts in 1900 and 1902 to approach the Local Government Board for local urban powers did not get the same support from Ruislip and Eastcote as from Northwood and there was a real danger that Northwood might feel inclined 'to go it alone'. Although historically Ruislip, Northwood and Eastcote had been within the same parish and the majority of the area in the same medieval manor, geographical features which were not conducive to good communication had tended to cause a social separation between Northwood and the other districts. This had been accentuated by the move to Northwood of new residents who did not come from the same rural background as prevailed in Ruislip and Eastcote and were resentful of the outlook and views of the more conservative rural communities.

By October 1903, differences were being overcome and a crowded public meeting held in Ruislip School passed a resolution with only seven votes against calling for the Parish Council to make application to the County Council for conversion to an Urban District under powers given by the Local Government Act of 1888. The application was successful and the County Council made an order creating the Ruislip-Northwood Urban District Council which was to be operative from September 30th 1904. This meant that the area now had a local authority which would be responsible for control over public health, the majority of highways and oversight over development.

One of the benefits arising from having an Urban Council was the appointment of a Medical Officer of Health, whose comments have been quoted in the first chapter. The authority was created at a time when local residents, both new and old, and local landowners were becoming aware of the potentials and problems of the pressure for new accommodation and it was advantageous that it was created in the same year as the Metropolitan Railway opened its extension to Uxbridge. The railway produced a new channel of direct communication from London into an area which was rural and isolated. It was also an area which had potential for the expanding middle classes who wished for modern accommodation away from the older central and eastern regions of London.

When the MoH started to make his examination of the RNUDC area he soon presented some rather unpalatable facts for the Council's consideration. He looked at drains; at water supplies; at incidence of notifiable disease; at population spread; at mortality and its causes and following the passing of the Housing and Town Planning Act of 1909 he was able to inspect living accommodation, report on existing defects and estimate the needs of the indigenous population. Some quotes from his reports which have been given in the first chapter show that he was not satisfied with all he saw. For the first time deficiencies in accommodation of people and the animals which served their requirements for food were exposed and published for the decision makers to see. It happened also to coincide with a demand for better town and suburban planning with the 'garden city' movement – as at Letchworth from 1903 – capturing the public imagination. Inspired by the example of Kings College who had drawn up a scheme for the development of its estates in Ruislip, the RNUDC applied, under the 1909 Act, to prepare a plan for the development of the majority of the land within its boundaries. Approval was given, and the final scheme which included

First steps in change

Houses in Bridle Road built 1912.

and modified that of Kings College at Ruislip was passed by the Local Government Board on September 7th 1914. The approved scheme formed the basis for the subsequent development of the RNUDC area for road type and dimensions; building densities; sanitary conditions and land use for housing, industry and amenity.

    One or two small areas were excluded from this plan as they were already being developed, and it is of interest to note that one of these was at Eastcote and was one of the spurs to create an overall area plan. The British Freehold Investments Syndicate, in addition to acquiring land by Northolt Junction station (now South Ruislip) were seeking to develop land on each side of the new halt at Eastcote covering the present Elm Avenue, Hawthorne Avenue, Lime Grove, Acacia Avenue, Myrtle Avenue, Beech Avenue, Oak Grove and Linden Avenue. From all accounts their main purpose was to sell plots of land without any control over the type of development which could follow. Their advertising was so successful that 650 plots had been sold along these roads between August 1909 and May 1910. Emphasis in advertising was placed on clean country air and surroundings as being good in themselves and presenting an ideal situation in which to bring up families. This is demonstrated by the road names which were allocated. The roads named after trees were meant to play on the town dweller's feeling that country life was so much better than life in town. Equal emphasis was not

Eastcote — From Village to Suburb

placed on the difficulties which clay soil would produce if not efficiently drained. Those with foresight in the locality were alarmed at the type of development which might occur if controls were absent.

Although plots were sold, building did not occur immediately. Before 1914 new houses at Eastcote were thin on the ground. Three new houses are recorded in 1909 and three more in 1910. Plans for 15 more were passed by the RNUDC by 1911; sewers were extended in Wiltshire Lane, Cheney Street and Bridle Road. A water main was extended partially along Elm Avenue. In 1912 it was reported that plans for 42 houses and seven additions had been passed for Eastcote. In the same year sewers were extended under Linden Avenue, Beech Avenue and Oak Grove. By now the layout of the 'tree' roads was complete. British Freeholds had agreed to deposit a sum of money with the Council to underwrite the cost of extending the sewer to their southern estate, an indication that the local authority powers now had 'bite' in them. The MoH's report of 1912 advised that as well as the British Freehold estate, Cheney Hill Estate, J. P. Page's Estate, the Imperial Estate and Woodland Avenue Estate were all being developed. Fifty four more house plans were passed in 1913. Development slowed with the moves to war in 1914, only eight plans being passed in that year.

Houses in Cheney Street built 1912-13.

First steps in change

Although various estates are recorded as being developed, such as the five mentioned in the previous paragraph, these should not be confused with the type of speculative building on the scale to be seen in the 1930s. A developer would lay out the road pattern of an estate, or would plan to develop ground along an existing road but he would not necessarily be the builder. Plots were sold and plans for buildings would be submitted individually at a later date. RNUDC Minutes from December 1911 to July 1913 record 16 applications for construction of houses or cottages, each application being for one or two dwellings. Twelve different developers submitted these plans through seven different agents or architects. In some cases the plans were for a personal dwelling and in other cases, the dwellings are clearly being built for sale or rent to third parties. The roads which were affected by these applications were Bridle Road, Cheney Street, Cuckoo Hill, Elm Avenue (sometimes called Elm Grove), Northolt Road (Field End Road), Lime Grove. It is not always easy to identify the precise date of development without looking at individual house documentation as planning applications, directories and Ordnance Survey maps do not always corroborate each other. For example, plans had been submitted to RNUDC between December 1911 and May 1913 for six houses in Bridle Road, in four cases for Mr H. Everitt with six plans being submitted through E. H. Appleton. Kelly's Directory for 1915/16 records five residents in Bridle Road yet the 6" to 1 mile Ordnance Survey map of 1916 shows no dwellings as having been built.

One major problem that was no nearer solution before 1914 was that of reasonable housing for labourers and the working classes. We referred to this topic in the first chapter by reference to the MoH's reports. Not more than 20 houses had been provided for the working class during the latter half of the 19th century and many were living in old stock which was in poor condition. Although still a rural area the population continued to grow by natural increase and immigration. To make matters worse, some farms and cottages were being converted to middle class use which inevitably meant lower density living for the middle classes and near over crowding for the poorer classes. Although Eastcote was not specifically mentioned, the MoH report of 1911 points to the evils of 'dual tenancies' which were found when inspections were made under the 1909 Housing and Town Planning Act. These were cases where a cottage would be let to two families with double occupation of kitchen, scullery and toilet, often resulting in it being the duty of neither tenant to keep these facilities and the surrounds of the dwelling clean. This shortage of cottage accommodation is mentioned annually and by 1913 the MoH is stressing an obligation on the Council to do something to rectify the problem. He estimated in that year that there was need for 20 cottages in Eastcote alone which would rent at no more than 6/- a week.

The theme was being stressed elsewhere during a series of

lectures which were given during the winter of 1911/12 at Benson's Hall (Old Barn) in the village. The lecture, as reported in the Middlesex and Buckinghamshire Advertiser of March 9th 1912, was given by Miss Churton of the Women's Industrial Council on the subject of the ideal cottage home. The audience included architects involved with local development. The address was concerned with standards of room size, number of rooms, heating, ventilation and lighting. Sanitation and food storage space were particularly commented on. Plans were shown and discussion followed. The chairman, Mrs George Edwards, had stressed the need for good cottages, in Eastcote in particular, in her opening address. Later she mentioned, as a member of the committee of the Ruislip Manor Cottage Society, the work that organisation was engaged on in seeking to rectify the problem in Eastcote, Ruislip and Northwood. They aimed to erect 100 workmen's cottages in the modern basic form which would rent at 6/- to 12/- (60p) weekly. She went on to say that the future might hold promise of cottages at 5/- (25p) a week. This particular society was an example of the types of voluntary organisation which had their roots in the awakening of social conscience in the latter half of the

25/27 Fore Street, built by Ruislip Manor Cottage Society in 1914.

First steps in change

19th century. These helped to satisfy a range of community needs which had been exposed by many writers, religious leaders, politicians and others aware of the social deficiencies suffered by many in the new urban industrial society. Nevertheless, some of the then current attitudes might not be shared by our egalitarian society of the 1980s. For example the following quote is taken from the Middlesex & Buckinghamshire Advertiser of May 4th 1912 when discussing the Ruislip Manor Cottage Society's activity in Manor Way, Ruislip:

"*It has been found to be the experience in all the new suburbs that have arisen on this side of London, that whilst plenty of effort is made to accommodate the middle classes, little or nothing is done for the working-class. There is consequently much hardship to the community generally. At places like Gerrards Cross, Beaconsfield, Farnham Common and Northwood, where there is considerable employment for chauffeurs, gardeners, carpenters and the like, there is extremely great difficulty for these necessary elements in the community to find housing accommodation; which again proves that no class can live unto themselves alone, and that any self-contained community must necessarily be composed of people of all classes.*"

Another point of interest is a comment at the Eastcote meeting by Mr Soutar of Messrs A. & F. Soutar who were consultant architects to the RMSC: "*in reply to a question,* [Mr Soutar] *said he found by his experience that when a bath was placed in the scullery, it was used for storing potatoes, and so on (Laughter).*" It would appear that greater emphasis was placed on satisfying and supporting the needs of the newer middle classes than of the older rural community.

At the Eastcote meeting a plan was shown by A. & F. Soutar of a field in Frog Lane, Eastcote where it was proposed to erect 42 cottages. These would vary in rent, dependent on position and size and would have gardens 25 feet wide and 100 feet in depth. Provision was also made for a tennis court. In May of the same year the Town Planning Committee of the RNUDC had met with the Ruislip Northwood Workmen's Housing Council – a pressure group who, encouraged by the MoH's criticism of the standards of cottages, were seeking to create a Cottage Society – and others to discuss the problem of the dearth of good working class accommodation. At this meeting, Alderman Thompson, Chairman of the Ruislip Manor Cottage Society announced their intention to build 32 cottages in Frog Lane and ultimately 100 in the Ruislip district. Plans were submitted to the Council during 1912 for cottage building and an extension of the sewer in Frog Lane. Unfortunately the First World War intervened before these plans could be finalised and, although cottages had been built by the Society in Northwood and Ruislip, only four of those planned for Eastcote had been completed by 1914. These still stand in Fore Street, one pair on each side of the entrance to Coteford Close.

EASTCOTE END

THE CITY MAN'S IDEAL

EMBRACE the opportunity now within your reach of securing your IDEAL HOME amid SURROUNDINGS OF UNSURPASSED NATURAL BEAUTY.

A VIEW ON THE ESTATE.

This Estate is within 70 yards of Eastcote Station, 12¼ miles from Baker Street on the Uxbridge line.

Shopping Centre in close proximity.

Fully and semi-detached freehold villas with every convenience, built in spacious grounds now for sale ready for immediate occupation.

Here you can have your own Tennis Court, Bowling Green and Garage.

Gas, Water and Electricity are at your door. Good metalled roads are already made.

Harrow, with its schools for juveniles, is quite close.

SAY YOU SAW IT IN "METRO-LAND"

106

PARK ESTATE

RESIDENTIAL SUBURB.

We have here, SITUATION, ARCHITECTURE, WORKMANSHIP, ECONOMY and FINISH to suit every requirement.

A PAIR OF SEMI-DETACHED HOUSES ON OUR ESTATE.

If you desire we can build to your own ideas and design.

Experts are available to advise you on any matter. Mortgages can be arranged.

We have a lifetime's experience in the building trade and are certain we can give you satisfaction.

NO AGENTS. Apply direct to:

TELLING BROS., Ltd.

ESTATE OFFICE, EASTCOTE STATION.

Telephone: PINNER 210. *Now read "Eastcote" Article on page 41.*

SAY YOU SAW IT IN "METRO-LAND"

107

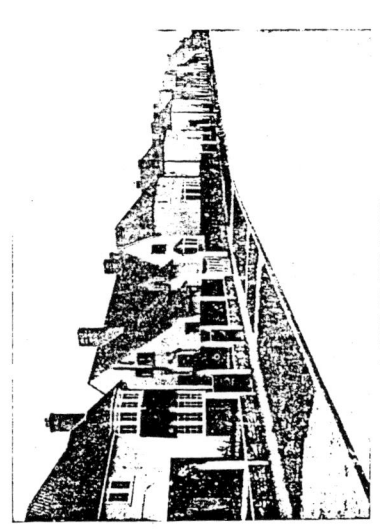

Eastcote End Park Estate, advertisement from "Metro-Land 1924".

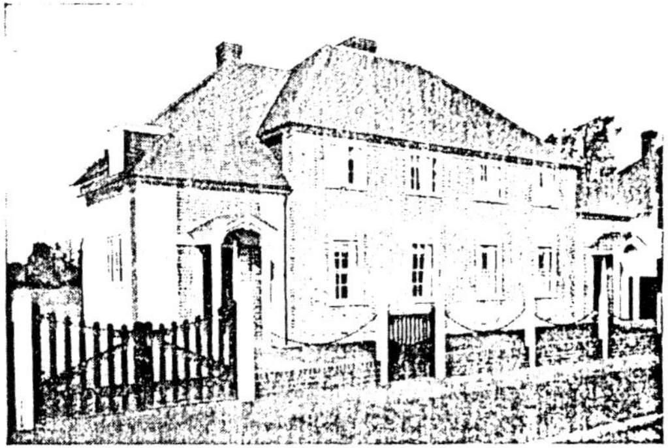

Chapter Three

"*London's latest ideal and picturesque residential district*"
— *1930s advertisement*

In 1918, fourteen years after the opening of the Harrow to Uxbridge section of the Metropolitan Railway with its exhortations from the Chairman and other dignitaries, suburban sprawl had not yet reached Eastcote. The village was still the main centre around which the old and new communities lived. Mrs Bennett Edwards was still resident at Haydon Hall, the Warrenders at High Grove, and tenants came and went at Eastcote House. Sir John and Lady Anderson were living at Eastcote Place (previously New House); Kenneth Goschen, a director of the Bank of England, lived at Sigers. (See note on Goschen at end of chapter). Field End House, Field End Lodge and The Barns were middle class residences having changed from their earlier farming connection and The Retreat had been erected behind Field End Villas. Mistletoe Farm and Hornend were also private residences and no longer working farms. W. J. Murch had moved from Field End Villas to Ruislip House in Field End Road (a substantial red brick house, now demolished and the site occupied by the road confusingly called The Sigers). Parts of Catlins Lane, Cheney Street and Bridle Road were developed and sparse building had occurred in the 'tree' roads nearer the station.

Ruislip Holt, previously a private house built in the mid-1890s and lived in by C. W. Millar (late of Sunnyside, Joel Street), had been purchased for St Vincent's Cripples Home and School for Defective Children which had commenced at Clapham Park. It had been formally opened for its new purpose in July 1912 by Cardinal Bourne in the presence of the Duke of Norfolk and other dignitaries. Children also continued to come to the Pavilion entertainment grounds, just south of Eastcote Station in Northolt Road, run by Arthur B. Bayly, for outings as thousands of others had before the War. Cyclists, ramblers and an increasing number of motorists came for summer day outings to the rural pleasures of Eastcote and continued to provide a seasonal income for the providers of refreshments. Cavendish Amateur Athletic Association had created their sports centre along Northolt Road before the War and were joined by others using the east side of Northolt Road below Woodlands Avenue.

Eastcote — From Village to Suburb

Shops were almost non-existent, but Alfred Button & Sons of Uxbridge had opened a grocer's shop in the village which first adjoined and then included the Post Office. Laundries, boot repairs, building and decorating trades were small scale in private hands with dairy produce being provided from the local farms and dairymen. Mrs Ward Dyer (nee Hinman) and others remember Mr Golding's milk round from Myrtle Farm, with his old style milk cart which contained the churn with tap. He also carried measures for milk to be poured into customers' jugs. Other requirements were obtained from Uxbridge or Watford or by delivery. Mrs Ratcliffe, who came to Coteford Close in 1919, remembers walking to Watford or Uxbridge to shop. There was no butcher in Eastcote, Crookalls being the nearest in Ruislip. Some older residents remember two calls in a day from the butcher – one for the order and one for delivery. Of course, not everybody could afford to buy meat. Eva Lavender, born in Ivy Farm in Wiltshire Lane, remembers the Lavender children walking to Northwood High Street for haircuts.

The Metropolitan Railway was the only public transport available. The most used roads might be metalled with gravel but hardly any were tarred. Main drainage had spread throughout the district as had the supply of mains water. Gas was supplied to the newer built up areas from the Pinner Gas Works and main electric supply from the Northwood Electric Company was available in the north of the district where they had run a supply to St Vincents. There was no street lighting although Northwood had started its own scheme before the War. Some of the bigger houses had their own private generating plants for the domestic supply of electricity; only a few had their own cars, motor cycles or a telephone. Apart from the few buildings already mentioned, Eastcote was still an area essentially agricultural in appearance with a very small and scattered population. Again, it was this isolation which was the main attraction for newcomers to the area.

Although there was a widespread housing shortage after the First World War, there were also shortages of supplies and of skilled workers, many of whom had been lost in the fighting. The election slogan of November 1918 – 'Homes fit for heroes' would be difficult to bring into effect, finance was short and controls were inevitable. Alan A Jackson in his fascinating study 'Semi-Detached London' explores the general situation at some length and mentions two pieces of legislation which were to bring a profound change in attitude towards the provision of housing, and to act as a stop gap to assist in a difficult period. The first was introduced by Dr Christopher Addison with his Housing and Town Planning Act of 1919 which put the onus of providing low rent houses on to local authorities with the support of an Exchequer grant towards the cost of such provision. The second was the Housing (Additional Powers) Act which granted lump sum subsidies to those who wished to build privately. The maximum which could be obtained under the latter Act was £160 for houses of 920 square feet, increased in 1920 to £260 for 1400

Eastcote Station looking towards Uxbridge, mid 1930's.

square feet. The main effect in Eastcote of this legislation was the development by the RNUDC of 34 dwellings in Coteford Close which took over from the development planned by the Ruislip Manor Cottage Society before 1914. Additionally there were a few new private houses which took advantage of the private subsidy. All building was, however, subject to the provisions of the RNUDC Town Plan of 1914. Further building by the RNUDC took place in the 1920s and 1930s with another 52 houses built in Fore Street and Wiltshire Lane. These have now been demolished and replaced by a new development which includes Everett and Wylchin Closes. A moment's reflection on the siting of these houses of the 1920/30s period shows them to be extensions of the village community but relatively distant from shopping and public transport facilities. Northwood Hills station did not open until 1933 and the bus route along Joel Street did not commence until after the Second World War.

The first major private development in Eastcote after the First World War followed the sale of the land along Field End Road to other builders. Part of the purchase was made by Telling Brothers Ltd, whose name was subsequently changed to W. A. Telling Ltd. Their development of the present Morford Way and Morford Close was to be significant in the change of centre of Eastcote as they also built the row of shops known as Field End Parade on the west side of Field End Road. These were built between 1924 and 1926, and are distinctive in their architectural style inasmuch that they are more closely associated with house design and less blatantly commercial than later shop building was to become. They can be easily identified as running between numbers 154 and 184 Field End Road. Close observation will detect a fractional difference in the facades of those to the north and south of Morford Way, as the latter include a patterned brick diapering at first floor level and might indicate that these were the first block to be erected. Some confirmation of this can be obtained from an advertisement in the June 1939 issue of the 'Aerial' of the Eastcote Association by Miss Clements, Ladies' and Childrens Outfitters, which claims this to be Eastcote's oldest business, founded in 1925. Miss Clements' business was in a double fronted shop (No 184), which projects out in front of the main building line. It is interesting to note the claim of 'oldest business' which emphasises the separation occurring from the older village community, which, of course, had older businesses.

Telling Brothers' estate was named the 'Eastcote End Park Estate', and Mr A. C. V. Telling advises that their development in Eastcote was limited to the houses in Morford Way, Morford Close and a few houses in the already laid out Hawthorne Avenue, Myrtle Avenue and Acacia Avenue. W. A. T. Telling Ltd later built a hall at the northern end of this parade of shops which Mr Telling feels was somewhat altruistically built as a Community Hall. In the late 1920s, however, the population of this new area of Eastcote was inadequate to support such a

"London's latest ideal and picturesque residential district"

venture, but in the early 1930s the building was converted into the Ideal Cinema. In the 1924 edition of 'Metro-land', the Eastcote End Park Estate was advertised as *'The City Man's Ideal Residential Suburb'*. Also *'Embrace the opportunity now within your reach of securing your IDEAL HOME amid SURROUNDINGS OF UNSURPASSED NATURAL BEAUTY.'* Detached and semi-detached freehold villas were available for immediate occupation with gas, water and electricity. Six years after the War, it was considered economic and expedient for gas and electricity suppliers to extend their main services. Alternatively, Telling Brothers offered to build to your own ideas and design. Tennis Court, Bowling Green and Garage were also available. Houses were sold direct by the builders who had their estate office at Eastcote Station. Telling Brothers' type of estate building was a compromise between the older concept of buying land and selling off plots (as had been done by British Freeholds before the war) and the new building which mainly preceded the buyer. Tellings offered both.

This estate was quite deliberately built as an almost self contained entity with transport immediately to hand (70 yards away), and in no way dependent on the old village community some three-quarters of a mile away. It was aimed at those who worked in London and wished to live in rural surroundings. It should be recalled, in imagination if not by memory, that this new community only had the scattered completed

Morford Way, built by Telling Bros 1924.

35

Eastcote — From Village to Suburb

houses in the 'tree' roads as near neighbours. Devonshire Lodge, a substantial detached house, had been built earlier in the century on the opposite side of Field End Road but apart from these the nearest building was Field End Farm to the north with The Pavilion and sports grounds south of the railway. All else was open fields. The first residents were, to a great extent, pioneers of the new Eastcote to come. And it came swiftly enough.

Three builders were mainly responsible for creating the 'new' Eastcote which developed to the north of the railway, expanding from the foundations laid by British Freeholds and Telling Brothers. These were Rotherham Estates Ltd, T. F. Nash and Comben and Wakeling. Each purchased part of the remaining Eastcote estates of R. Hawtrey Deane; Rotherham to the west of Field End Road and north of the Telling estate, Nash on the opposite side of the road. Comben and Wakeling purchased the freehold of Eastcote House, its grounds and land bounded by Chapel Hill, Bridle Road, Cheney Street and the High Road from Cuckoo Hill to the village. Rotherham and Nash were each to call their estates 'The Deane Estate' and Comben and Wakeling named their's 'The Eastcote Park Estate'. There were other smaller builders and some larger firms who continued Nash and Comben and Wakeling's work and created the complexes north of Bridle Road and east of Cheney Street; the Mount Park estate north of the village and developments along Joel Street. The effects of the work of the main three named should, however, be considered separately.

Plan of Rotherham Estates' Deane Estate.

"London's latest ideal and picturesque residential district"

Rotherham Estates who were first off the ground laid out Meadow Way, Crescent Gardens, Deane Way, Maple Close (earlier to be called Field Close) and extended Hawthorne Avenue to meet Deane Way. Nash commenced operations soon afterwards, setting out Abbotsbury Gardens, Devonshire Road, Lowlands Road, Deane Croft Road, Rushdene Road and The Chase. Comben and Wakeling planned St Lawrence Drive, Burwood Avenue, Pamela Gardens, Rodney Gardens and The Glen. The final layout of the Eastcote Park Estate was not decided until the mid 1930s as a lengthy local dialogue went on concerning the future of Eastcote House and its grounds after Comben and Wakeling had purchased the Hawtrey estate in 1930. The original plans had been to demolish the house and walled garden and sweep a forty foot road round so that it would have extended the present Rodney Gardens to the west over the site of the dovecote and then bring it south to the present entrance of Pamela Gardens from Chapel Hill. They had also planned that the land on each side of the River Pinn should be an open space. The dialogue was finally concluded in 1937 when the local authority purchased Eastcote House and 9.1 acres of ground for the use of local residents. In the meantime Comben and Wakeling had altered their layout to the present routes of Pamela Gardens and Rodney Gardens.

The modus operandi of these speculative builders is of interest. They aimed their products at a different market than that of earlier developers. The 1914/18 war had accelerated the move towards smaller families among the growing army of white collar workers. This relatively new socio-economic class did not aspire towards having domestic servants, even if these had been freely available and within their means. They also, like the more affluent upper middle classes before them, began to wish for ownership of a wider range of the newer consumer goods and services. The majority had no history of home ownership, living mainly in rented accommodation in the older suburbs of London and Essex north of the Thames. London and the South East did not experience the extremes of hardship which resulted from the 1929/31 economic depression. Additionally, London as a growing commercial centre experienced immigration from Scotland and the provinces of those transferring to new administrative and managerial posts.

To attract these prospective clients, the speculative builders sought to produce a package deal which offered a modern house which, with all the modern conveniences of gas and electricity would be clean and easily run and have adequate accommodation for a family of two parents and one or two children. The package also offered simplicity of legal procedure and finance and was presented in such a way as to bring it within the means of these potential clients. Roads were made up with adequate walking pavements, and street lighting and all main services.

In 1930 T. F. Nash was advertising his estate at Eastcote as being *"Three minutes from the Station. Only Half-an-hour from City and*

Eastcote — From Village to Suburb

Hawthorne Avenue, 1930.

West End, yet in the Country." The same advertisement offered six different types of detached and semi-detached houses priced from £1325 down to £895. There were no road charges, legal fees or stamps or mortgage charges. By 1934, Nash was advertising eight different types ranging in price from £1050 down to £715. Deposits for purchase ranged down from £75 to £40 with a 24 year mortgage arranged with weekly repayments reaching from £1/6/- (£1.30p) down to 17s 10d (89p). At this time the average income for white collar workers might be within £5-£9 a week with skilled manual workers coming up to £3-£5 a week. Not only did these builders have to convince the potential client of the economic viability of such a purchase, but in many cases sought to alter the habits and traditions of a lifetime and background. To this end extensive advertising campaigns were mounted using up to date promotion techniques.

Roads were laid out before building commenced and then specimen pairs or individual houses were erected. These were furnished by local or large retailers, gas and electric light companies. They were then presented as the show houses to give an idea to purchasers for comparison with their own housing. Well trained sales personnel were always present and the estate office would have plans of the full estate divided up into plots and full details of types of houses and possible

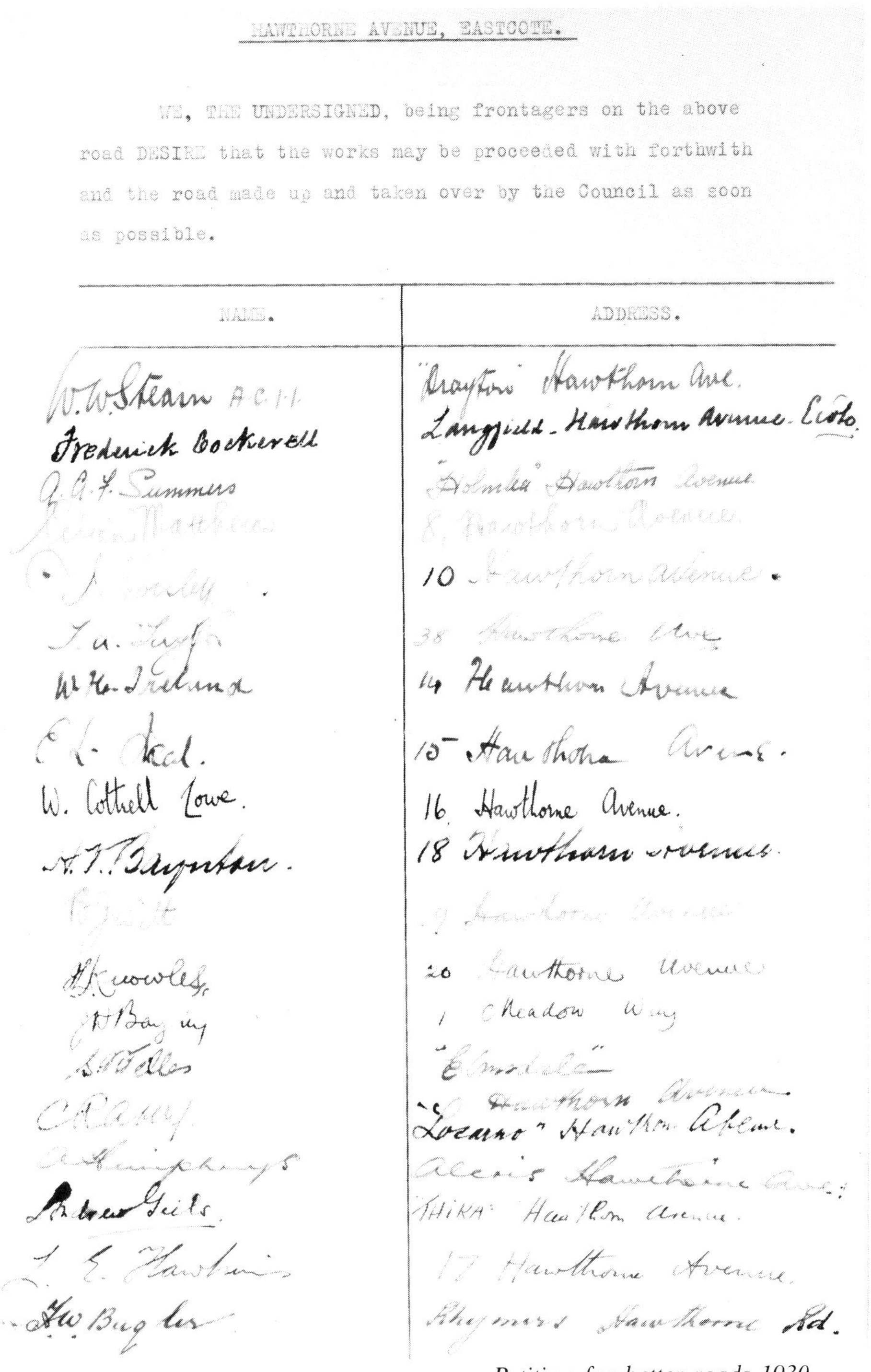

HAWTHORNE AVENUE, EASTCOTE.

WE, THE UNDERSIGNED, being frontagers on the above road DESIRE that the works may be proceeded with forthwith and the road made up and taken over by the Council as soon as possible.

NAME.	ADDRESS.
W. W. Stearn A.C.I.I.	"Drayton" Hawthorn Ave.
Frederick Cockerell	Langfield. Hawthorn Avenue. E'cote.
J. A. F. Summers	"Holmlea" Hawthorn Avenue
(illegible)	8, Hawthorn Avenue.
(illegible)	10 Hawthorn Avenue.
J. A. Tuff	38 Hawthorne Ave.
W. H. Ireland	14 Hawthorn Avenue
E. L. Neal	15 Hawthorn Avenue.
W. Cothell Lowe	16 Hawthorne Avenue.
A. T. Brynton	18 Hawthorn Avenue
(illegible)	19 Hawthorn Avenue
H. Knowles	20 Hawthorne Avenue
H. Bay*(?)*	1 Meadow Way
S. Wells	"Elmsdale"
C. Remy	Hawthorn Avenue
A. Humphreys	"Locarno" Hawthorn Avenue.
Andrew Giles	"Alexis" Hawthorn Ave.
L. E. Hawkins	"THIKA" Hawthorn Avenue.
A. W. Bugler	17 Hawthorne Avenue
	Rhymers Hawthorne Rd.

Petition for better roads 1930.

39

Eastcote — From Village to Suburb

modification. Garages were normally an optional extra in an age when private car ownership was low, but garage space was always offered by these three main builders. The Metropolitan Railway assisted by offering subsidised fares. For example, season ticket rates to Liverpool Street were for three months first class £6/16/-, third class £1/15/3. Cheap rate workmen's fares were available before 7.30 a.m. At Eastcote the buyer could be shown that there were two railway services – Metropolitan to the City and District (Piccadilly from 1932) to the West End. A purchaser would choose the type of house and location on the estate and a prospective completion date of about four to six weeks would be suggested. Decorations could be chosen from a select list. Having chosen one's site and type the purchaser could visit periodically to observe progress. In the interim the purchaser could if he wished select furniture, curtains, carpets etc from the store who furnished the show house. Inevitably, there was this extra expense, as in addition to a fair amount of curtaining needed for the quite high proportion of window area, existing furniture suited to more old fashioned housing would be out of proportion in the new house. In any case, there were schemes available whereby new furniture could be obtained on easy weekly payments. In fact, it was all too easy for purchasers to find themselves building up a sizeable weekly payout with mortgage payments, hire purchase for furnishing and rental for cooker. Fortunately, those moving into the Eastcote estates were usually able to use their occupational business acumen to avoid these pitfalls, but there were always tales current of those who curtained and furnished the front rooms whilst leaving the back rooms empty.

Meadow Way, a Rotherham Estates development.

"London's latest ideal and picturesque residential district"

The author's first house, in Eastcote. Deane Croft Road, 1932.

Deane Croft Road, 1986.

All three builders aimed to keep their estates up to the standards which would be attractive to middle class purchasers. They either built detached or semi-detached houses – no terraces. All were provided with 30 feet or wider frontages with building at a density of no more than eight to the acre. Hedgerow trees and shrubs were largely grubbed out for building purposes, but trees were planted along roads. Comben and Wakeling did manage to protect some larger oaks, two of which remain today, in St Lawrence Drive. They avoided long rows of houses by planning short curving roads, small greens and a greater variety of types than the other two builders. Rotherham staggered the building line and both they and Nash incorporated some prestigious houses. Rotherham have four of these in Meadow Way at the junctions of Crescent Gardens and Maple Close. Nash had four larger detached houses on offer with a price range from £1500 to £5000. Two of the former are in The Chase and one in Lowlands Road. Three larger detached houses were built by Nash facing on to Field End Road running north from Deane Croft Road. The first at the Deane Croft Road corner was a doctor's residence and surgery and that next to it was occupied by T. F. Nash's mother in 1932 and later by his brother. One of the £5000 type was built beyond this and lived in by T. F. Nash himself. All of these, including the replacement for T. F. Nash's house destroyed in 1940, were demolished when Winslow Close was developed in the 1960s, and it is ironic that these latter factory prefabricated buildings had a shorter life

41

than those which had been built in the 1930s. At the time of writing (1987) Winslow Close is being developed by Bovis as The Forresters. Later T. F. Nash was to move to a larger house he had built in Bridle Road, which now forms the core of Missouri Court.

When Rotherham had completed their Deane estate they moved their operations to extend North View into Eastern Avenue. This was done in two moves, firstly the part within the RNUDC area which includes North View, Boldmere Road, Boundary Road, Chandos Road and Ivy Close. The continuation of North View into Eastern Avenue was within the Urban District of Harrow and should not strictly be considered in this study of Eastcote. However, the building of the first part virtually completed the majority of the development of Eastcote immediately north of the railway. Nash also opened up Cannonbury Avenue from Rushdene Road but this also goes east over the RNUDC border. Neither Nash nor Comben and Wakeling finished their estates. By mid to later 1930s builders wished to move to other areas and would sometimes sell off the remainder of their estate to obtain finance for other operations. In the case of Nash parts of Deane Croft Road, The Chase and Rushdene Road were built by S. G. Nash, his brother, or by A. G. White, his son-in-law. The differing external designs can normally be easily identified. The Eastcote Park Estate was completed by C. V. Galley. The latter tended to concentrate on bungalows and these are in evidence in Rodney Gardens, St Lawrence Drive and part of Bridle Road where 'Sigers' used to stand. Except for Rotherham's Deane Estate, building had not been fully completed by 1939.

Although a slower starter, the land south of the railway began, from the mid 1930s, to change from sports fields, clay pigeon shooting range and pig farms to be broken up by bricks and mortar. Woodlands Avenue was laid out for development before 1914 but only a handful of houses materialised. It is of interest that at Rayners Lane, Eastcote, Ruislip Manor, Ruislip and Ickenham new building commenced on the north side of the Metropolitan Railway before that on the south. The older village communities in each case were on the north side; the River Pinn likewise. The southern area was on lower ground than the north and earlier impressions were of wide open windswept areas. Some residents of the older village community described the southern area as 'the Bogs.' More important factors in the twentieth century involved availability of main supplies of drainage, water, gas and then electricity. These invariably had their origins on the north side. The Pavilion, with 32 acres of sports fields, had been in existence for the majority of the century and had been the Mecca for thousands of children in day parties organised by schools and churches in inner London. There are still many living in Eastcote whose earliest recollection of the district was from such visits. The variety of organisations who had sports fields and facilities south of the railway found access easy by the Metropolitan and District lines.

"London's latest ideal and picturesque residential district"

Changes commenced in the mid 1930s. The district retained its popularity for residential purposes and as land had mainly been taken up north of the railway, pressure was directed south particularly as George Ball's large Manor Homes estate commenced and flourished south of Ruislip Manor station. Properties built on the south side tended to be cheaper and smaller than those to the north of Eastcote. A variety of builders were drawn to this part including Davis Estates Ltd, W. G. Estates Ltd, G. T. Crouch Ltd, Taylor Woodrow and Vincent Estates. From 1935 Davis started to exploit the old Pavilion grounds which had now fulfilled their original purpose. They built Ferncroft and Greencroft Avenues and Broadhurst Gardens with the current fashion of 'sun-trap' design. On the opposite side of Northolt Road, which had been renamed Field End Road as a continuation of the northern stretch, was an estate of contrasting mock Tudor style meant to appeal to those with a sense of history. This contained Aragon Drive, Cardinal Road, Castleton Road, Seymour Gardens, Cleves Way and Essex and Garth Closes. Clearly the developers were going for the 'all-out' picture of nostalgia.

The Davis estate was almost completed by 1939. The planning of this estate merits attention in view of the methods used by Davis to obtain the best benefit from the existing landscape. Houses are well spaced and boldly placed and the open space with trees in Greencroft

Field End Road, shopping centre at time of Silver Jubilee 1935.

Eastcote — From Village to Suburb

Avenue gives a 'garden city' suburb aspect. As well as building houses, Davis were the first to introduce large scale bungalow development in Pavilion Way at the south end. Whereas today bungalows command a premium in their selling price, this was not the general case in the 1930s. They were built as smaller houses and these of Davis as well as those of Galley on the Eastcote Park Estate are two of the three main areas of deliberate planned bungalow development in Eastcote. The south side of Southbourne Gardens had been completed and parts of Pine Gardens, but the 'Tudor' estate had not been completed, neither had the north and south legs of Woodlands Avenue or their interlinking roads. Whitby Road had been driven through to join with Victoria Road thus joining Eastcote and Ruislip Manor with another road link. The Manor Homes portion of this road was completed but that in Eastcote awaited completion after 1945. Southbourne Gardens joined up with Chelston Road of that estate and with Oak Grove at the old British Freeholds estate. Similarly Linden Avenue was extended to Victoria Road.

The other part of Eastcote to be built over was to the north of the village itself. W. Spencer Ltd built the Mount Park estate with Mount Park Road, Wentworth Drive, Gerrard Gardens, Tudor and Sutton Closes. This estate involved the demolition of Fore Street Farm with Wentworth Drive taking the place of the footpath right of way over Holder's field which had previously joined Fore Street with Joel Street. This development differed from the other estates in Eastcote as there was a mixture of bungalows, four-house terraces and two storey maisonettes. The building of this estate completed the encirclement of the old village centre by 1930s bricks and mortar. To complete the pre-war picture in that locality we should note the erection of *'A Garden Estate at Eastcote'* in 1935 on the eastern side of Fore Street where Smith Brothers built some houses at £665 which included *'marble Bath and separate WC'*. Their advertisement went on to advise that £5 would secure a property which would then cost only 17s 6d (87.5p) weekly to purchase or 21s (£1.05p) weekly to rent. The Spencer estate to the north of Wentworth Drive in Coniston Gardens had to await completion until after 1945.

During the period between the two World Wars interesting conversions were carried out at 'The Grange' in the High Road and to Cheney Farm. The Ideal Home magazine of August 1925 gives a good photographic coverage of 'The Grange' conversion showing how the barn which ran in line with the old house was joined to make one building. The original doors of the barn were removed to produce the archway which can be seen from the High Road; two floors were inserted into the timber-framed barn to provide day and night nurseries in the upper floor. Two new dormers were inserted into the barn and the whole exterior was weatherboarded to match the old house. Whilst the conversion was under way, two old fireplaces were revealed in the dining room and the drawing room.

"London's latest ideal and picturesque residential district"

Eastcote Park Estate, October 1933.

A full coverage of the Cheney Farm conversion was given in Homes and Gardens in November 1934. In this case an entirely new block was added to the original building, this being at right angles to the old farmhouse which is end on to the road. The rough cast wall finish with fascia timbers matches in well with the older building, and has tiles which were taken from the barn which was demolished. To connect the new and old portions inside, a gallery was formed at first floor level. Modern services were incorporated into the building and the conversion gave the benefit of 'old world' charm married into and accentuated by new construction. In each of these conversions particular attention was paid to the exterior so that, from the outside, the finished appearance is of one building and, in each case, pleasing to the eye.

One of the major criticisms which were directed against the new 'dormitory' suburbs springing up around London was the lack of facilities and that they did not form a natural community. The matter of community organisations will be dealt with in a later chapter, but with regard to services, there was no shortage in 'new' Eastcote. In the early part of the 1930s development, Rotherham Estates built a further block of shops in Field End Road, opposite to the Field End Parade of Tellings, and named it Devon Parade. It is an easily identified block between 177 and 195 Field End Road. It had the merit of creating a two-sided shopping centre and was sufficiently spaced away from the opposite shops to enable Eastcote to arrive in the 1980s with a wide road throughout its shopping centre which avoids the congestion found in other centres. In 1935, T. F. Nash built a further block, Deane Parade, between Deane Croft Road

45

and Abbotsbury Gardens to replace the stabling he had used to service the building of his estate. A little earlier another block was being built between 161 and 171 Field End Road, and around 1936/7 Devonshire Lodge was demolished and a further parade of shops built from Abbotsbury Gardens to join up with 161. An individual insert block, represented by the present 173/5 was then built to house J. Sainsbury Ltd, grocers and Walton (London) Ltd, fruiterers. After 1935 Station Approach was built by T. F. Nash between North View and the station terminating at the footpath to the car park. Queen's Parade opposite was built at about the same time. Telcote Parade had already been built south of the station and just before 1939 the quadrant of shops at the junction (north side) of Elm Avenue and Field End Road was built. In 1932 there had been 26 shops in Field End Parade; by 1939 the number of businesses in the shopping centre was 105. In 1932 there had been a representative group of types of shop with one of each trade, but by 1939 there were 10 grocers, 6 butchers, 5 fruiterers, 4 bakers, 4 fishmongers and fried fish shops and 3 dairies. In 1932 there had been a music salon which sold pianos, sheet music etc. This had gone by 1939 but instead there were 2 radio shops. As another commentary on the times, there were two private circulating libraries where the normal charge for borrowing books was 2d a volume a week. The only county libraries available were after school hours at Cannon Lane School and Coteford School in Fore Street. Multiple stores were well represented; as well as Sainsbury and Walton there were branches of Westminster Wine Company; Watford Cooperative Society; J. H. Dewhurst Ltd.; United Kingdom Tea Co.; Fifty-Shilling Tailors; Tesco Stores Ltd.; Eastman and Son, cleaners; Sanders P thers, grocers; F. W. Woolworth & Co. Ltd.; Walton, Hassell and Port, grocers; Bata Shoe Co. Ltd.; Truform Boot Co.; Boots the Chemists; Sketchley Dye Works Ltd.; Express Dairy Co. Ltd.; W. H. Smith & Son Ltd. and United Dairies (London) Ltd.

By 1936 local traders felt themselves to be in a strong enough position to form their own Chamber of Commerce as opposed to belonging to any of the neighbouring Chambers. They proved their point as by 1946 their Honorary Secretary Noel Frewin, who was a partner in the opticians practice in Queen's Parade, when writing an article on progress for "The Aerial" claimed that they had nearly achieved 100% membership amongst local traders. He went on to outline some of their functions – pressure for amenities such as public conveniences; demands for better telephone provision; complaints from and about local traders; offering advice on the many regulations operating; character of the shopping centre; goods displayed on pavements; closing hours; parking etc. They also ran social functions and money raising events for charitable causes. An outstanding earlier example of this latter activity was on the occasion of the Coronation of George VI in May 1937 when they organised a coach outing to the cinema for children from St Vincent's

"London's latest ideal and picturesque residential district"

Deane Parade, Field End Road.

Hospital. Those children who were unable to take part were not forgotten, as a party was given in the wards together with two demonstrations of a television set by Mr Gillett. As 'The Times' reported *"....probably the first to introduce this latest achievement of the age to a hospital ward."* The author recalls personally attending television demonstrations at Mr Gillett's shop, and it would not be stretching the imagination too far to assume that author and children saw demonstrations of the same set.

The inter war period had witnessed the almost complete transformation of Eastcote from a small country village to a new type suburb with a radical shift in the main centre and a change of services. The population of Eastcote at the beginning of the century had been just under 600. By 1939 it was close to 15,000 with the majority of this increase occurring within 9 years. As a large proportion of the new Eastcote wage earners worked in London, the expectations of the directors of the Metropolitan Railway had been fulfilled by 1939. Traffic increased but there was mounting criticism of travelling conditions during the rush hour periods. Travel by rail remained relatively inexpensive but conditions could demand the adoption of a Spartan attitude. At the peak of the morning rush hour City trains could be full before reaching Rayners Lane. That district which also experienced an unprecedented population explosion, contributed a further travelling quota to almost full carriages. Metropolitan trains were still using the earlier compartment rolling stock, and feet needed to be kept tucked under the seat when six to ten were standing between the five each side who were seated. A continuing complaint was the termination of a proportion of Metropolitan Line

47

Eastcote — From Village to Suburb

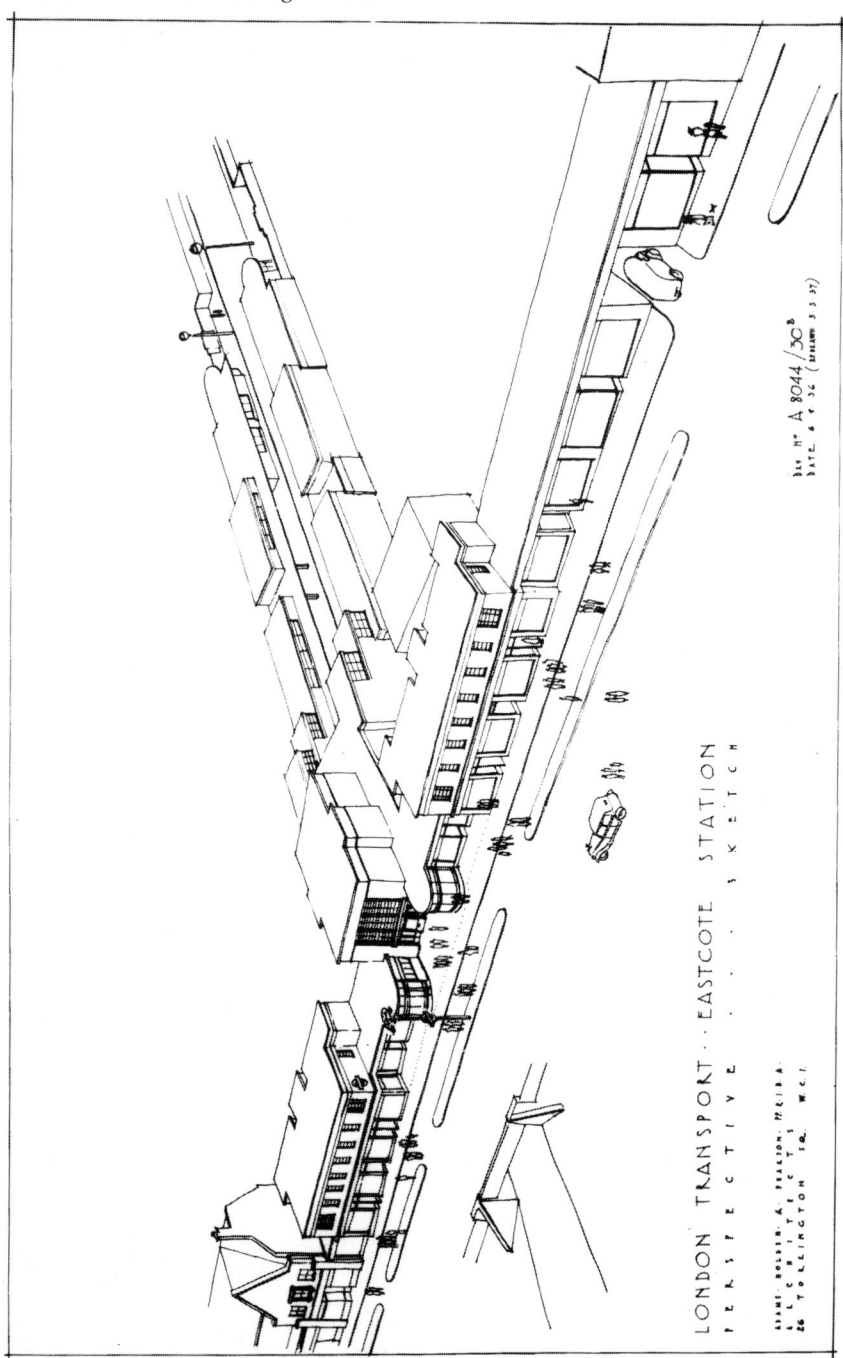

Projected plans for Eastcote Station 1937.

"London's latest ideal and picturesque residential district"

trains at Rayners Lane station which was exposed to southerly and south westerly winds in autumn, winter and spring. Similarly, bus routes did not multiply in line with the increase in population. The only services prior to 1933 were the LGOC route from the Red Lion terminus at Pinner to Uxbridge Garage and the 'Royal Highlander' route from Pinner to the 'Eight Bells' at Uxbridge. These were combined just prior to the London Passenger Transport Board being created. There was no bus route from north to south of Eastcote or to Northwood until after 1945. On the other hand, ten minutes' walk to the station was considered as close proximity to a generation which owned few private cars and was more used to walking or cycling. When railway stations were designed, including that at Eastcote in 1939, provision had to be made for cycle accommodation rather than car parking space.

This chapter has been devoted to the physical changes which occurred on the green fields of Eastcote, and has attempted to give an insight into the types of people who came to settle in their thousands. However, such extensive change in a short period of years does not necessarily produce an instant social community. The next chapter will look at the social institutions which also developed.

Eastcote station c. 1947.

Eastcote — From Village to Suburb

Note. *In earlier works on Eastcote, Kenneth Goschen has been described as Governor of the Bank of England. However, Edwin Hartley, in the Spring 1956 number of "The Aerial", points out that Goschen was related to a Chancellor of the Exchequer. Further research shows that Kenneth Goschen was the nephew of George Goschen, Chancellor from 1887 to 1891 and 1st Viscount Goschen after 1900. Kenneth's father Charles Hermann Goschen became Chairman of Lloyds as well as having other interests in the City. Kenneth, his uncle and his father were all Directors of the Bank of England.*

Incidentally, the Parliamentary association with this immediate locality was continued after the Second World War as the house built alongside the site of the old Sigers was occupied by Maurice Webb who was, for a period, Minister of Food in the post war Labour government.

Chapter Four

Churches, Clubs and other Social Centres

At the beginning of the 20th century, Eastcote only had one church, the Wesleyan Methodist in Chapel Hill, four inns or beer houses, an Institute for social gatherings, a cricket team and a football team. The parish church was at Ruislip. The Methodist Chapel would only accommodate about 150 but it was not licensed for marriage services until 1934. Burials took place at Ruislip until the new cemetery became available at Northwood in 1914. The village children went to school in Ruislip at the National School which stood in Eastcote Road, by the side of the present Manor Way. Alternatively, they could use the school in School Lane, Pinner or from 1910 could attend the Council School in Pinner Road, Northwood. All of these schools have been demolished. These facilities had to serve the spiritual and social needs of Eastcote residents apart from the one-off social events which were organised at Haydon Hall, High Grove or in the School's buildings from time to time. It does not require a great effort of imagination to judge that a scattered rural population, worn out after heavy manual work and faced by journeys over unmade roads, would not have been clamouring to go to many outside activities once the autumnal rains set in.

This state of affairs did not continue, however, after the middle class newcomers of 1910 to 1925 settled in. These new Eastcote residents moved quite deliberately to savour rural atmosphere, but with outlooks and attitudes shaped by the urban revolution of the later 19th century. They were able to live in rural isolation, but in an encapsulated urban style, with such material possessions as were deemed to be necessary. This grouping was distinctly separate from the 'villager' born in the locality of working class stock. The newcomers brought their material comforts with them and were able to create their own social pleasures. It was this group who were mainly opposed to the 1930s expansion when they saw the rural ambiance which they had moved to enjoy, gradually disappear. They looked with horror at the demise of the fields and hedgerows and objected to requests for such amenities as street lighting because these would be representative of the urban areas they had left behind. They did, however, expect roads to be properly maintained. We can easily sympathise with these feelings. In our own time objections are often raised when there are moves to build more houses. Many see this is a dis-enhancement of the locality by increases in

51

density of buildings, population and traffic. Not only did these middle class newcomers spring to the defence of the geography and way of life of the old village, but they were also to bring about the creation of social institutions which we accept today as being part of the normal community background. Part of their protest included the formation of the Eastcote Association (later to be the Eastcote Residents Association) in 1930 to try and prevent the extension of the 'new' shopping area northwards along Field End Road. This attempt was unsuccessful, but the Association continues to act as a guardian of social values to the present time.

By 1939, Eastcote could be said to have three distinct populations within its boundaries and these did not combine on many levels to form a total community. Each of these three – the villagers, the early 20th century immigrants and those coming in the 1930s – came from fundamentally different backgrounds with differing traditions and ways of life. The villagers were not a static closed community but in many cases had common links of family and work. The first newcomers were from solid middle class background and the third group were often being introduced to home ownership for the first time and in the main were individual families without previous links, except by accident. By all accounts the villagers were fairly passive recipients of the major changes which took place around them. In some cases they regretted the passing of the old ways but generally they were more pragmatic in their attitudes. They did not always contribute to the philosophy of 'the good old days' because they had experienced the deficiencies of early 20th century rural life, and were eager to accept any benefits the new society brought with them. They did not necessarily mix freely with the newcomers but retained their own community links.

Those who came after 1918 often saw themselves as protectors and enhancers of the village. They also tried to fill the gaps which they saw as missing in local social institutions. The Eastcote Village Institute had flourished as a social centre since 1893, supported financially by the more affluent families. Two of the earlier middle class families were to have a hand in the maintenance of older institutions and the creation of new ones for the villagers. By chance, these two families lived opposite to each other in Cheney Street – the Philips who took over Hornend in 1910 and the Hinmans who moved to 'Fyvie' by the side of the river in 1919. Around 1920 George Philip senr. sponsored a move to replace the old Institute building, then in some dilapidation, and a new building was erected in Fore Street with improved facilities. The old 'tin hut' which had been used in the village was re-erected behind the new building. Among other activities within the new building were meetings of the Girls' Friendly Society which was attended by village girls and others in domestic service in the locality. Mrs Margaret Ward Dyer remembers her mother returning from a meeting of this society one evening and being full of enthusiasm for its replacement by a Women's Institute. This was founded in May 1924 with the support of ladies of the district including

Churches, Clubs and other Social Centres

Mrs Philip, Mrs Hinman and Mrs Crane (all of Cheney Street) and with Mrs Vivian of Field End House acting as first president. Meetings were initially held at St Lawrence Church Hall in Bridle Road and then transferred to the Institute building in Fore Street.

It has been mentioned earlier that the parish church was St Martin's, Ruislip. In 1913 an acre of ground had been purchased from Mr Hawtrey Deane by the Bishop of London's Fund, but progress towards establishing an Anglican church in Eastcote was hindered by the advent of the 1914/18 War. Further support was forthcoming after the War from a group headed by Mr and Mrs Kenneth Goschen of 'Sigers' who embarked on a series of sales, garden parties and similar events. On December 18th 1920 a Mission Church was dedicated. In 1921 a further one acre of ground was given to the church by Mr Hawtrey Deane and by 1925 over £3000 had been raised towards the church, sufficient not only to pay for the Mission Church but also to provide a parsonage bungalow leaving over £1000 towards a permanent building. The Mission remained under the jurisdiction of the Vicar of Ruislip and was served by priest missioners. In the mid-1920s plans for a permanent building were produced by W. A. Forsyth, a local architect. These were not approved by the Bishop of London, however, and the local congregation had to wait until the London Gazette of November 13th 1931 published a scheme which, according to the Silver Jubilee booklet, proposed that the Mission District *'shall become and be constituted a separate district for spiritual purposes and that the same shall be named the parish of St Lawrence'*. Sir Charles Nicholson was commissioned to draw up plans for a permanent building and on December 10th 1932, R. Hawtrey Deane laid the foundation stone. The church was consecrated by the Bishop of London, the Rt. Rev. A. F. Winnington-Ingram on October 21st 1933. The last priest missioner appointed, who was to become the first Vicar of Eastcote, was the Rev. R. F. Godwin, who remained in Eastcote until his retirement in 1956.

We have seen that the village had the oldest religious body, the Methodist Church. This congregation had its origins in a group formed by Adam Clarke in 1826 on his own estate at Haydon Hall. Dr Clarke was a leading Methodist theologian and had been three times President of the Methodist Conference. Following the deaths of himself and his son, it was no longer possible for the congregation to continue there. Miss Winter, a friend of Mrs Lawrence of Field End House, provided funds for a simple chapel to be built in that part of Field End Road, which became known locally as Chapel Hill. This chapel was opened in May 1848 and services were held there until the first part of the present building in Pamela Gardens was opened in 1951. Post 1930 new residents, therefore, had a choice of the Anglican church in Bridle Road and a non conformist chapel near to the village. The increasing number of new residents also contained some of Roman Catholic persuasion. Miss Eleanor Warrender of High Grove had been the benefactress for the

53

Eastcote — From Village to Suburb

founding of the Catholic church in High Street, Ruislip in 1921. This was the local RC church for Eastcote residents but it became apparent that there was a need for a centre for services in the immediate locality. Services were initially held from 1934 in Field End House which was in the possession of the Grail community. A chapel of ease, known as the Chapel of the Blessed Thomas More was soon established under the jurisdiction of the Ruislip church and the first Midnight Mass was sung there at a crowded service in January, 1935. A permanent building was opened and blessed by Bishop Myer in May 1937. That building is now used as the church hall.

The last of the major churches to be established in Eastcote pre 1939 was St Andrew's Presbyterian Church of England. Among the newcomers to Eastcote and Ruislip were a number of Scots and others with a Presbyterian or Congregational background. In addition, the General Assembly of the Presbyterian Church of England had taken note of the suburban expansion and had purchased a plot of land in August 1937 at the junction of Bridle Road and Rushdene Road, just within the RNUDC eastern boundary. The land was purchased from T. F. Nash (Investment) Ltd and A. G. White Developments Ltd for a total sum of £852.10s. This site price can be compared with the price paid by the Methodist London Mission and Extension Fund for their present site at the junction of Field End Road and Pamela Gardens in 1935 when they purchased it from Comben & Wakeling Ltd for £750. Even in the 1930s these prices were low, indicating that developers were conscious of the need for social amenities and were prepared to sell for such purposes below the normal building value.

After the site had been purchased, a meeting was convened by the Church Extension Committee of the North London presbytery of the Presbyterian church to sound out the viability of such a project. Sufficient interest was indicated for a small group to commence services from May 1938, the venue being Eastcote House. In addition a Sunday School was commenced with 6 children. By March 1939 enough progress had been made for an interim session to be appointed to administer this new 'Preaching station'. By May it had been agreed to raise this to a 'sanctioned charge' under the title of St Andrew's. Plans were drawn up for the erection of a hall which could be used for services on Sundays and social activities during the week. It was visualised that this would be the hall of the permanent church building to come sometime in the future. In spite of the year being 1939 with ominous clouds of war piling up on the horizon, the group went ahead with fund raising activities, one being a Garden Gift Party at Hornend in Cheney Street. The owners were the same Philip family who had been benefactors to the old village by assisting with the move of the Village Institute and the commencement of the Womens Institute. The building of St Andrew's was completed so that dedication and opening of the Church Halls was able to take place on November 11th 1939. The Rev Dr Thomas Walker, an Old Testament

Churches, Clubs and other Social Centres

scholar with a reputation as writer and lecturer, had agreed to be minister-in-charge for 12 months or the duration of the war, whichever was longer. He probably never visualised that he would be there until 1947.

Steps were also taken in this post-war period to provide for other types of social activity. The villagers already had their football and cricket teams dating back to the 19th century. Their membership slowly increased as a few newcomers to the area joined their ranks. Lawn tennis was becoming a favourite summer sport for younger members of middle class families. The Eastcote Lawn Tennis Club was founded by Mr Lee in 1925 on land adjacent to his own house 'Sunnyside' in Joel Street. This club has been successful and still functions strongly at the present time. This was not the case with similar ventures. It will be remembered that the Ruislip Manor Cottage Society had made provision for a tennis court in their pre-war plans for Fore Street (Frog Lane). This did not materialise but another did when Telling Brothers developed their Eastcote End Park Estate. Tennis courts were provided with a pavilion behind Field End Parade shops to the north of Morford Way. The 1932 Kelly's directory lists it as the Eastcote Country Club. This venture did not survive for many years and neither did the Sylvan Lawn Tennis Club in Catlins Lane which was listed in the 1924 directory. Mention has already been made of the hall built by Telling Brothers which it was hoped might act as a community centre for the 1920s newcomers. Mr E. S. Hartley writes in his 'Eastcote History' published in the Eastcote Residents Association 'Aerial' in Spring 1956 that the hall had a spring oak floor and a large stage and that some performances were given there by musical and dramatic societies from Ruislip and Harrow. The venture did not prosper in that form, however, and the building became better known to post 1930 residents as the Ideal Cinema which continued until its ultimate closure in the early 1960s.

It was the boost in the population after 1930 which gave the impetus for more social and spiritual centres, although the proportion of the total population which used them was relatively small. We should recall that the new residents moved into new houses and whilst the age of DIY had not yet been born, they were faced with the sometimes unfamiliar tasks of gardening and some home maintenance. Most of those who were to be confronted with these new duties worked in London leaving Eastcote before 8 a.m. on six days a week, not returning until 6 p.m. or later on five of those days, and working half days on Saturdays. The fact of being in an unfamiliar area with these new commitments of travel and home tasks did not leave a lot of time for joining social organisations. The younger members of these families did not have the home jobs and were those most likely to join and form new bodies. So we find the birth of another new lawn tennis club in Lowlands Road in 1933 catering almost exclusively for those living in the surrounding new

Eastcote — From Village to Suburb

St. Lawrence's church at time of construction, October 1933.

houses. Again, this club has continued to flourish up to the present time, though the clubhouse had to be replaced after a fire in 1983.

The middle 1930s were to see further growth of organisations and opportunities for leisure activity. Just over 10 acres of ground from the High Grove estate were acquired by the RNUDC from Miss Warrender for use as a recreation ground with entrances from Lime Grove and Myrtle Avenue. These were laid out in 1935 and in the same year a gift was offered and accepted by the RNUDC in the form of a pair of fine wrought iron gates for use at the Lime Grove entrance. The gift came from the Eastcote Association through their secretary C. J. Carter. The gates, which still stand, are of interest inasmuch that they were originally erected at the end of the 1870s at the private art galleries of Thomas Agnew and Sons in Bond Street. A little later the Council constructed tennis courts in the Recreation Ground for public use, and a sandpit and children's playground were provided. Eastcote Recreation Ground has now been renamed Warrender Park which may or may not be an improvement.

The Eastcote Bowling Club was also formed in 1934. Although the Cavendish Pavilion and Sports Ground were still in private ownership the club were able to make use of their bowling green. The club was well supported from the beginning but catered mainly for the

Churches, Clubs and other Social Centres

new Eastcote residents. In this case, however, there was a mixing of the firstcomers with the 1930s residents. A further addition to the new centre of Eastcote was a new pub 'The Manor House' (now the Berni Steakhouse). This stood alongside Ideal Motors and the Ideal Cinema, the three forming a distinct central complex. As the villagers had the Black Horse, the Woodman, the Ship and the Case is Altered it was becoming apparent that the two communities were developing separate social facilities, particularly at the adult level.

There should have been more opportunities for children and youth of the older and newer communities to mix together at schools and youth organisations both spiritual and secular. When the Institute building in Fore Street was purchased by the Middlesex County Council Education Committee in 1927 to open as an Infants School, this was the only school available in Eastcote. Up to this time, the situation was exactly as it had been at the beginning of the century except for the additional facility of the Council School in Pinner Road, Northwood. The other school in Eastcote Road, Ruislip had to cope with the increase in population of both Ruislip and Eastcote and by 1929 the accommodation was inadequate. In 1931 the Bishop Winnington-Ingram CoE School was opened on the same site with room for 280 pupils. The Manor Secondary School had opened in 1928. This latter school was to take the senior pupils from the church school, but itself had to be extended in 1936. Again it was the new area of Eastcote which was to benefit from new school building when the MCC opened Cannon Lane Primary School in Cannonbury Avenue in 1934. The complementary secondary school, Pinner County School was opened in Beaulieu Drive in 1937. Although these two schools are not in Eastcote, the policy of the County Education Committee at that time was to provide area schools. The Primary School catered for the needs of the younger children of the eastern side of Eastcote north of the railway as well as those from the rapidly expanding area towards Cannon Lane, and the County School for the senior level. Many older children went by scholarship to County Schools in Uxbridge, Harrow, Wembley and Ealing, but the 1930s also witnessed an increasing demand for grammar school type education from the growing ranks of middle and lower middle class families. This resulted in some children being sent to the many private schools offering this type of education – at a price. None operated in Eastcote, but were to be found in the surrounding districts. A generation grew up who became familiar with the use of public transport from an early age, so developing an independence which would not have been possible elsewhere in the country.

Children and young people tended to associate mainly with those who lived in their own immediate locality or those with whom they travelled to and from school. Mixing of the three communities at school age did not, therefore, automatically occur. Parental choice of school and general oversight of social activities sometimes had the effect of accentuating the segregation.

Eastcote — From Village to Suburb

Those who lived on the newly developing estates had a variety of interesting activities available on their own doorstep. To live in the heart of an area which was being built up was a unique experience for these children. Building activities hold interest for all age groups but the children of the 1930s estates also had immediate access to building materials as well as watching the operations of building. Possibly because parents were busy settling in with the variety of new domestic tasks, those on the new estates allowed their children more freedom than would have been customary in longer established communities. These children were often freer than their parents had been to explore all of their surroundings and embarked on a remarkable self education experience. Fields which were in the ownership of builders but not being developed were there for exploration, walks and games. Easier relationships grew up between the "new" children and as confidence developed the areas to be explored assumed wider bounds. This was also the age of the cheap bicycle and with little traffic on local roads these same children explored areas at a distance from home not dreamed of by their parents in their own childhood. Not only were fields ready to hand but Ruislip Woods, recently made available to the public were within walking distance. Also nearby were the delights of Ruislip Reservoir (now the Lido), and the viewpoint of Haste Hill.

Organised activities, in the form of Scouting and Guiding encouraged these desires for a minority but organisations for the younger age groups, outside of the Sunday Schools, were few in number in the 1920s and 1930s. It should also be remembered that this period saw a continuing fall away from attachment to churches and again the Sunday Schools, of which the Methodist was the strongest, were only attended by a minority of children. The annual Sunday School outing and Xmas party were often a spur to join for the required minimum period of attendance. Very few children expected to continue at college or university before 1939 and the majority left school between 14 and 17 to obtain employment and join their fathers in travelling to London. A few, particularly girls, went to commercial colleges to learn additional skills such as typing, bookeeping and shorthand to equip themselves for the increasing number of jobs in London offices. An interesting insight into geographical behaviour has been told to me in this connection by Eva Lavender, who was born in the village and lived there for the whole of her childhood. It was not until she left school at Ruislip and went to Clark's College at Ealing that she used Eastcote station for the first time. The demand for mobility was less at that time, but was more common to the life styles of the newer residents. It would be very wrong to generalise on this point as some living in the older village did travel to London and elsewhere for employment, but in the early part of the post 1918 period there was less tendency for the older village community to make regular use of the new transport facilities provided by the Metropolitan Railway.

Churches, Clubs and other Social Centres

This came with the 1930s newcomers even if only measured by sheer weight of numbers.

We are drawing near to the conclusion of this survey of social institutions created before 1939. However, it should be noted that the men's section of the old Village Institute were to have yet another home when in 1938 under the chairmanship of George Philip, they moved into a renovated stable block of Eastcote House. Eastcote House was to become increasingly a place where meetings could be held as has been seen with the early Presbyterians. The 1st Eastcote Scout Group met there for a period before the 1939 War, as did other organisations. Two further Women's Institutes were founded, Field End in 1937 and South Eastcote in 1938. By 1939 Eastcote had not only been created as a new suburb of mainly owner occupied houses with a balanced shopping centre, 4 churches, a cinema, 5 public houses, two tennis clubs, a cricket club, football club and two residents' associations (the Eastcote Park Estate Association having been formed in August 1937 to ward off the threat of creating St Lawrence Drive into a main road into Joel Street); it had also become a new form of community with a new geographical centre, the old village having been almost completely submerged. The June 1939 issue of the Eastcote Association's 'Aerial' offered other suggestions for leisure hours including British Red Cross Association, Chess Club, Choral Society, Coronation Players, Camera Club, Eastcote Players, Fencing Club, Keep Fit classes and a Rambling Club. Haydon Hall had passed from private ownership into local authority ownership in 1937 and Bessingby Recreation Ground, shared by residents south of the railway from Eastcote and Ruislip Manor, had been almost completed by 1938. So that all age groups could be catered for, 'Eventide Homes' for the elderly had been built in Fore Street in early 1939. A complete residential suburb had been created, arising outside of the old village centre, without any industry except for service facilities such as garages and still retaining the smithy in the old village centre.

Eastcote — From Village to Suburb

War Memorial.

Chapter Five
Eastcote in Wartime

As anybody over the age of 45 knows by personal experience, the effect on a community of either of the two world wars of the twentieth century was widespread and, in many cases, personally shattering. During the First World War, Eastcote was still mainly a village with newcomers beginning to settle around its periphery and with some attempts at new settlement around the Metropolitan station. It was the first major war to involve the civilian population in all spheres of life. It is true that in the nineteenth century civilians had their worries during the Napoleonic wars when invasion was threatened and during the Boer War when nationalism and the growing casualty rate brought a degree of social involvement such as the British population had not previously experienced. Nevertheless, the First World War brought a much greater awareness of the nastier aspects of war, particularly after 1915 when it was clear that the probable length of the war would be greater than originally anticipated and when civilians could see casualties with their own eyes.

The main effects of total warfare were death and casualties, deprivation of food and other items normally needed for everyday life, limitations of social activities and changes to social organisation. 134 men of Eastcote joined the Forces; it is not recorded how many women worked in industry, transport and communication or in H.M. Forces. Sixteen names are recorded on the Eastcote War Memorial. The names are representative of all walks of life and include villagers and newcomers. Casualties were too often seen as the war progressed and not only within families. Mr and Mrs B. J. Hall of Field End Lodge gave over their house as an auxiliary hospital, and many wounded passed through those doors. Eastcote Lodge in the High Road was used for a period to house German officer prisoners-of-war and in November 1914 Belgian refugees are recorded at Southill House. Although not in Eastcote, it would not be possible to ignore the close proximity of Northolt Aerodrome. Originally proposed as a flying club, by 1915 it was a fully operational military airfield. By September 1915 air raids on London were commencing and military aircraft were kept on standby at Northolt to attempt to repel the raiders. Northolt was also used as a training squadron but in these early days of flying casualties could arise from technical faults as much as from enemy action. There are two recorded incidents at Northolt in 1915 and 1916 where aeroplanes which took off to intercept German raiders crashed almost immediately after take-off. Similarly, Capt T. H. Bayetto, who is buried in St Martin's, Ruislip and is commemorated on the Eastcote War Memorial is recorded as having died as a result of a "fall whilst flying in an aeroplane." Northolt was to cause other worries for the MoH of RNUDC during 1915 when he commented in his Annual Report on the inadequate drainage system at Northolt Flying Ground which ran in shallow grooves over clayey fields producing abominable smells in summer. As a result of this complaint filter beds were established at the Flying Ground by 1916.

Another result of air raids on London is mentioned in the MoH report of 1917 when 40 cases of overcrowding are recorded in the RNUDC area during the August raids of that year. Although the MoH annual reports are much abbreviated during the wartime period – Dr Hignett himself was on active service and Dr R. Ritchie of Northwood was the Acting MoH – it is possible to obtain some information about the district. Clearly, house building had been reduced to a minimum and there were severe restrictions on commodities for all but essential work. However, progress was made on another matter of great social importance. It will be recalled that in the early years of the century infant mortality and deaths during childhood were at a high level. In 1917 a Health Visitor was appointed to assist mothers with children's welfare. As would be expected, there was initial opposition but her persistence and persuasion overcame this and she made 668 visits from February to December to homes in Ruislip and Eastcote. As a sign of things to come, the same year saw the establishment of baby clinics at Ruislip and Northwood. One of the major factors which assisted the move towards her acceptance was a measles epidemic when 202 cases were recorded at the Ruislip and Northwood schools. Unfortunately, the whole district was to experience the great influenza epidemic during the last 3 months of 1918 when 9 deaths resulted.

In terms of numbers and widespread effect, it was the Second World War that had the greatest impact on Eastcote. We have seen in earlier chapters how the district grew in population, houses and social amenities. By September 1939 the newly created suburb was beginning to become established although many residents had only recently arrived. The situation was not any different to that of any other newly developed district which had not integrated itself fully into a self-sufficient community. Not only had residents to become accustomed to restrictions on their way of life but many were to be uprooted for membership of HM Forces, voluntarily or compulsorily, and were drafted to a variety of other parts of the country or indeed to other parts of the world. Families who were left behind were often not yet familiar with their new home districts. There was a temporary end to home buying and new houses were initially left unoccupied. Some shops in the new centre were empty, in particular the newly-built part of Orchard Parade from "The Manor House" up to the present Post Office. Some community projects had to be halted. The 'Advertiser and Gazette' issued September 8th 1939 noted that the contract for the first part of the new church hall at St Lawrence was to

1940 Air Raid Incident Map.

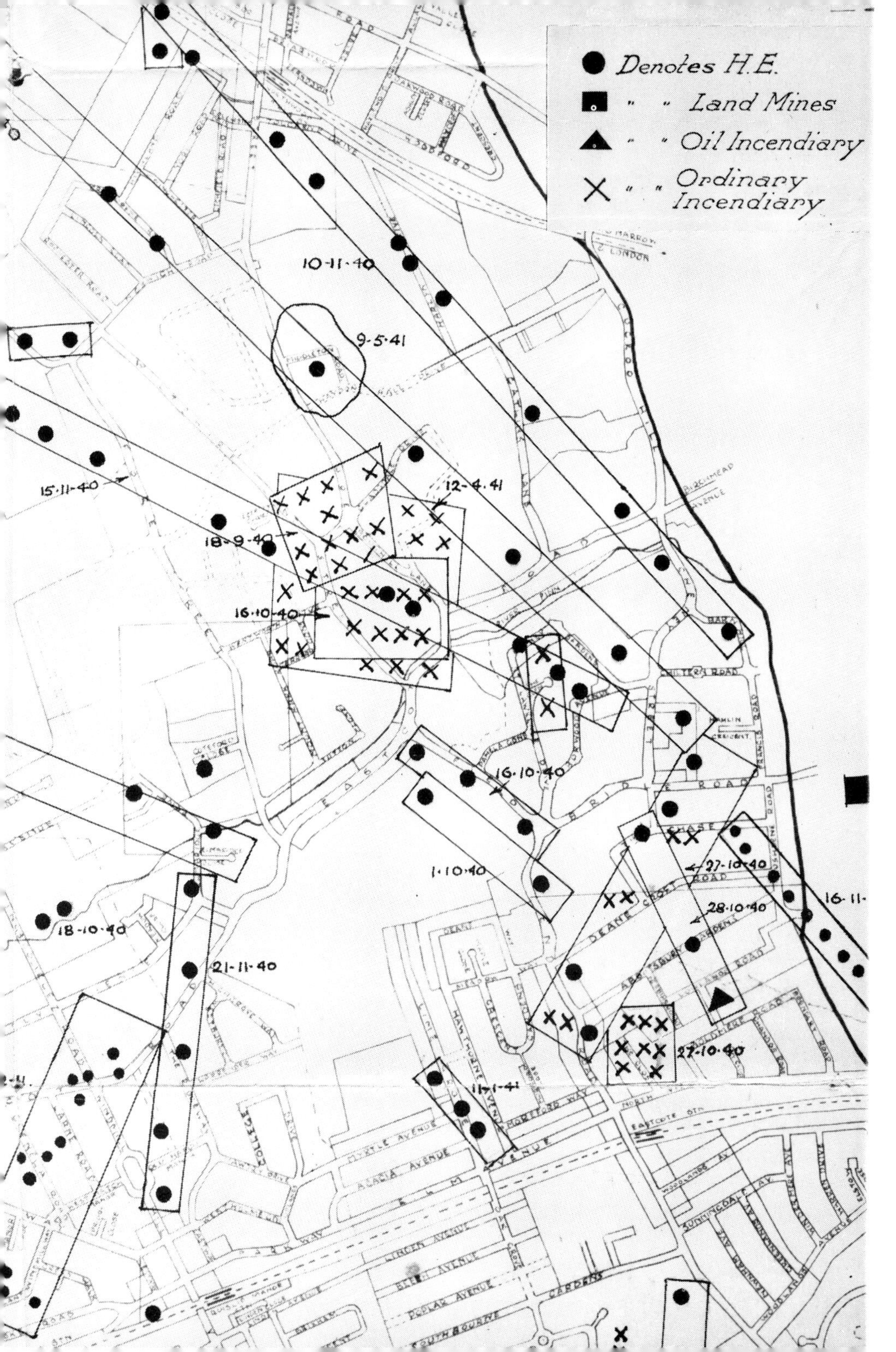

have been signed that week. The issue of September 15th recorded that the Trustees of the Methodist Church were to have met to make a decision on the tender to be accepted for the new building to be erected on the corner of Pamela Gardens, but the meeting was postponed. As mentioned in the previous chapter the new buildings for St Andrew's Presbyterian Church would not be ready for dedication until November.

Many people in 1939 were not surprised when war was declared even if they regretted it and were in a state of apprehension. The Munich Crisis of September 1938 had to some extent prepared people and communities for the events of 12 months later. In 1938 they had been forced to face the possibility of an all-out aerial attack being launched upon them and had commenced to think of taking steps to counteract such an event. Some recalled the bombing of London in the First World War; others were aware, at second hand, of the bombing which had taken place in China, Abbysinia and Spain. Imaginative previews of the 'blitz' had been made in the film 'The Shape of Things to Come' and newsreels at cinemas left an uneasy feeling for many. Preparations for such an eventuality had been taken in 1938 with the issue of anti-gas respirators for all age groups; trench-type air raid shelters had been dug and vulnerable buildings of strategic importance had been sand-bagged. Air Raid Precautions (ARP) organisations had been instituted in 1937. The legislation authorised local authorities to set up an establishment of paid personnel for dealing with fire, rescue, demolition, first aid and ambulance services together with the administrative services necessary to support these. Defence against air attack, which would include the building of shelters and the creation of a nationally recognisable warning system, had also to be organised. The RNUDC were the local body responsible for many of these precautions and they set up their ARP Control Centre in the cellars of Haydon Hall, Eastcote. As gas was forecast as being a major weapon of aerial warfare, community defence against this had to be made as well as distributing personal respirators. To assist with this, two Decontamination Centres were built in Eastcote – one between the shops of Station Approach and the station itself, and another in the grounds of Haydon Hall. Both still survive; the one by Eastcote station was used for many years after the war by Eastcote Timber Supplies.

Following the signing of the Munich Agreement in September 1938, people resumed their normal lives, tensions were relaxed, defence organisations saw a decrease in manpower and there was a slackening of controls. The Eastcote Association, in the 'Aerial' of June 1939, reported that they were concerned about the condition of the trenches provided behind the shops of Devon Parade which had been dug hastily in the preceding September but which were becoming unsightly and waterlogged. The Council had assured them that tenders for making good all trenches throughout the district had been obtained and that work would proceed. The same issue reports an ARP Display which had taken place

Eastcote in Wartime

on June 10th in Eastcote when fire fighting equipment was demonstrated. A half page article reported on a garden fete held in the grounds of High Meadow, Catlins Lane as an opening activity of the newly formed Eastcote Refugee Committee whose purpose was to provide temporary hospitality in this country for refugees from Europe prior to their migration to the USA. A page and a half was given over to a gardening article which led up to the use of lawns for clock golf, badminton or deck tennis. Organisation reports looked forward to an expansion of activities in the coming seasons, better street lighting was called for and attention was directed to the new decorative shrubs and trees to be planted behind the station platforms. The general tone and content of articles did not appear to anticipate the approach of a six year war to commence 3 months later.

    The awakening came on a sunny Sunday, September 3rd when the Prime Minister, Neville Chamberlain made a broadcast to the nation advising them that they had been at war with Germany since 11 a.m. Although the country was prepared for air raids, few expected the sirens to give warning within 10 minutes of the broadcast. Reactions varied from disbelief to horrified anticipation. Those at church services behaved differently from church to church. The 'Advertiser and Gazette' records that the Vicar of Eastcote just caught the last boat train back from Amsterdam and conducted the morning service through to the end despite the air raid warning. The Methodist service was shortened after the preacher was made aware of the warning and the congregation dispersed into the bright sunshine either to go home or find shelter somewhere, with the option of remaining within the building. From the preceding Friday, mobilisation of the Forces had taken place, a blackout on all lighting at night had been imposed and ARP personnel had been called to their posts. The ARP Control Centre went back to Haydon Hall for the opening months of the war, later moving to Northwood, and air raid wardens were on duty at their local centres and posts to be ready for any emergency. They immediately had to enforce lighting regulations. Apart from initial reactions to the declaration of war, the restrictions on lighting were the most irksome for people to get used to. Not only did darkness in the street bring unexpected hazards, and an increase in road accidents, but it was some time before the meaning of a complete blackout was understood. There were those who thought drawing curtains was enough, others overlooked the point that unless guarded against, opening a front door could cause a beam of light to be thrown forth. In addition, wardens' warnings were not always received in the best of spirits, particularly if people took umbrage at a near neighbour having authority to enforce regulations on them.

    As well as having to find blackout material for all windows and doors families safeguarded their houses against the danger of flying glass from blast damage by criss-crossing each pane of glass with gummed paper strip. Households were also expected to have first aid equipment to

Eastcote — From Village to Suburb

hand and, hopefully, some means of extinguishing fire. Very few individual households had their own personal shelter. The 'Anderson' shelter made of curved corrugated iron sheets could be erected in a garden, but distribution of these was limited. Few could afford an underground shelter, but as time progressed more houses did endeavour to have some kind of shelter, some of which remain to this day. Most families selected a strong point for a shelter within their houses, either beside the party wall or under the stairs.

Fortunately the first siren warning was a false alarm. Two further alarms, both false, came firstly during the early hours of Monday, September 4th and secondly on Wednesday morning, September 6th. This latter warning coincided with early morning travel to work. The station closed and trains stopped running for about 2 hours. Under the heading "Eastcote's First Traffic Block" the 'Advertiser and Gazette' gave an account of the congestion at the station after the All Clear sounded when all those who wished to travel to London arrived at the same time. London Transport were, however, congratulated for extending the period during which cheap 'Workmens' tickets could be purchased.

Residents' social life was disrupted further by the ban imposed by the Government on the opening of cinemas or public attendance at football matches etc. This ban was lifted after two weeks and those who chose to go to the Ideal Cinema on Sunday, September 17th could see

Decontamination Centre remaining in Haydon Hall grounds.

Eastcote in Wartime

'Oh, Mr Porter' with Will Hay and company, or on Monday, Tuesday and Wednesday following, 'East Side of Heaven' featuring Bing Crosby and Joan Blondell; Edward G. Robinson in 'A Slight Case of Murder' was the second feature. On Thursday, Friday and Saturday came 'The Little Princess' starring Shirley Temple with the Jones Family in 'Everybody's Baby!' The Ideal had an outsize tarpaulin erected to act as a light trap and performances were timed to conclude by 10 p.m. Among the churches, St Lawrence Church decided to move Evensong forward to 3 p.m. and St Andrew's Presbyterian Church arranged for Sunday evening services to be cancelled and held an alternative afternoon service. The Methodists also changed their evening service time and for a period in late 1940 held services in the Ideal Cinema.

Communal surface shelters and trench shelters were gradually provided throughout the district including a trench system behind the east side of the shopping parade on the site of part of the present car park, and another brick shelter in front of Deane Parade. There was another surface shelter at the end of Woodlands Avenue. Outside Field End Parade was a Police telephone box with a high level air raid siren. Wardens' posts were created in local areas, often in garages or erected on island sites on greens left on the new estates as happened in St Lawrence Drive. Following the early alarms and anticipation of the worst possible occurring, the so-called 'phoney war' followed until late Spring of 1940. The greatest frustrations were found when travelling or shopping. London Transport covered the windows of their trains and buses with netting which later had a small area cut away so that travellers could see where they were. Lighting within coaches was initially by a small blue bulb which made it virtually impossible to read a newspaper or book. Added to the frustrations of travelling in near darkness, not knowing where one was unless stations had been counted, was the cold and snowy winter of 1939/40. Not only were journey times doubled or more, but concern was felt at the 'firework' display given off by conductor shoes of trains having difficulty in penetrating the frost or ice cover. Unkind thoughts were expressed when a journey was prematurely terminated at Rayners Lane station and all were ejected. On at least one occasion passengers 'mutinied' and a Piccadilly Line train was forced to continue through to Uxbridge.

Shopping was frustrating due to shortages and price increases. As early as September 15th, 1939 the 'Advertiser and Gazette' was reporting dissatisfaction in Eastcote at the varying level of sugar prices. As the central London fish market was dispersed it also reported that an Eastcote fish trader was forced to send a lorry to Colchester and back – 120 miles – to obtain supplies which would normally have come from Billingsgate. Argus, the Ruislip-Northwood correspondent of the 'Advertiser and Gazette', was reporting in December on the shortage of torch batteries in shops even though new torches inclusive with batteries were plentiful. From January 1940 the housewife also had to contend with rationing of various foods. Although many grumbled at this restriction it was generally agreed that the system was fair. It involved registering for meat and groceries at specific shops nominated by the consumer and change could only be authorised by the Food Control Office. This latter, which was responsible for issue of ration books, was installed at Eastcote House.

The 'phoney war' was rudely interrupted in April, 1940 when the Germans invaded Norway and the British expedition sent to prevent this failed. Worse came on May 10th when German forces invaded the Low Countries. Set back followed set back with the success of the German blitzkreig on land through Holland, Belgium and France resulting in the evacuation of the British Army from Dunkirk from May 29th and the capitulation of France on June 20th. In May, Anthony Eden, Minister of War, announced the formation of Local Defence Volunteers (later renamed Home Guard) in every town and village. Volunteers came forward in large numbers and over the next few months Eastcote residents became used to seeing road blocks mounted for the purpose of examining identity cards by members of their own local branch. During July and August of a very fine summer the South East of England and East Anglia were the main recipients of the German onslaught on aerodromes to cripple the RAF prior to an attempt at land invasion. Although there were fewer aerial combats over Middlesex than over the southern counties the display was still impressive and awe inspiring.

For air defence purposes the country had been split into Fighter Group areas, each Group being further divided up into Sectors. The main Filter and Control Room of Fighter Command was at Bentley Priory, Stanmore. Number 11 Group which covered the whole of South East England to just beyond the Isle of Wight, the southern half of East Anglia and the Home Counties had its Operations Room at Uxbridge. Sector Z from Northolt covered the northwest corner of 11 Group. Although local residents were not aware of the facts, Spitfires of 609 (West Riding) Squadron had been in action over Dunkirk from May 30th to June 2nd accounting for 7 German planes destroyed but with the loss of 5 of their own pilots. The same squadron also acted as escort for Winston Churchill when he paid two visits to France during June. In January, 1940 Group Captain S. F. Vincent was appointed Commanding Officer of Northolt and was responsible for a unique form of camouflage for the airfield. He felt that as it was situated in a partially urban area it would more easily merge into its surrounds if camouflage took note of this. Group Captain Vincent persuaded those responsible to make the hangars look like double rows of small houses by the alternate pitched roofs being painted bright red with cream facings on the sides broken up by mock painted windows and doors. Other painting was done to give the impression of gardens with a painted 'meandering stream' on the main runway to complement the rural side of the airfield. It is estimated that

Eastcote in Wartime

over a fifteen month period, approximately 4000 bombs dropped within a two mile radius of the airfield with only two recorded main incidents at the airfield itself. Northolt was responsible for the Sector Operations Room which was sited originally at the aerodrome, but in May 1940 was moved to eventually occupy two small shops immediately on the north side of Ruislip Manor station. As facilities became inadequate there, the Operations Room was moved into Eastcote Place. This was a very closely guarded secret and few local Eastcote residents were aware of the move. King George VI visited the Operations Room at Ruislip Manor on one occasion and it is suggested by one source that as Winston Churchill was prone to visit the Operations Rooms from time to time he may also have visited Eastcote Place. The Barns in Field End Road was also used for RAF personnel.

The official map of incidents during the 'blitz' shows 18 raids to have taken place between September 8th 1940 and May 9th 1941, which resulted in bombs of various types being dropped within the Eastcote district. These were mainly high explosive bombs of varying size with 106 of these being dropped evenly over Eastcote. In addition, there were fairly heavy concentrations of incendiary devices over the area around Haydon Hall with other scatterings on the Eastcote Park Estate, The Chase, Deane Croft Road, The Close, Devonshire Road, each side of Pine Gardens and to the south of the Yeading Brook. Two of the more dramatic incidents – and this must be qualified by saying that all incidents were dramatic to those immediately effected – resulted from two land mines dropped on October 16th 1940 with virtually no casualties and earlier in the same month when a 'stray' drop caused the complete demolition of T. F. Nash's first residence in Field End Road with regrettable and appalling casualties to the residents of the house. One of the land mines fell where Bridle Road meets Eastcote Road, Pinner, just over the RNUDC boundary, destroying five houses and badly damaging others in the vicinity. It also caused considerable damage to the newly erected St Andrew's Presbyterian Church. The RNUDC Golden Jubilee Commemorative Booklet records the other landmine falling through the roof of a house in South Eastcote, coming to rest in a downstairs room alongside a bed under which a mother and two children were lying but no harm was caused. They were shocked but unharmed. The same booklet records that over the whole RNUDC area there were a total of 57 air raids with 241 high explosive bombs, over 2000 incendiary bombs and 4 land mines dropped by parachute. Later in the war five flying bombs affected the district, but none of these, fortunately, dropped within the Eastcote area. As a result of these raids 27 people were killed and 231 injured in the RNUDC district.

The Golden Jubilee Booklet states that nearly one third of the buildings in the whole District suffered damage, and from the proportion of bombs falling, Eastcote suffered a good share of this. Even St Vincent's Hospital experienced the effects of three 500lb bombs straddling it,

Eastcote — From Village to Suburb

demolishing the chapel but remarkably causing no casualties. Deane Parade shopping parade had one shop, Gillett Electrical and Radio Ltd, demolished with attendant damage to neighbouring premises, one Sunday evening late in October 1940. Fortunately the proprietor and his wife were visiting a neighbouring flat at the time and escaped physical injury. First aid repairs were done to most damaged properties within a short time but in some cases re-erection had to wait until after 1945.

Eastcote is not an industrial district but some of the empty shops in Deane Parade and the new Orchard Parade were taken over by Mr H. H. Kerswell who ran a temporary wartime industry making camouflage material and netting. He later set up in Deane Parade packeting concentrated soups etc. having transferred the whole camouflage business to Orchard Parade. Other rural-type industries developed as a result of the increasing spread of food rationing. Local restrictions on keeping of live-stock were lifted to permit householders to keep chickens and goats in their own gardens. Certain controls were retained over these, particularly where somebody had sufficient chickens to sell eggs to others, in which case the number of people who could register with these 'home' producers was limited. Foodstuff for fowls was also limited and many kitchens – and whole houses – were perfumed by the smell of mash being cooked. Food shortages also prompted many to grow vegetables in their gardens. Lawns were dug up and very few thought of installing the garden games mentioned in that gardening article in the June 1939 'Aerial'. Another by-product of food restrictions and the Government's campaign 'Dig For Victory' was the formation in September 1940 of the Eastcote Allotment Association. In April 1942 the title was changed to Eastcote and District Horticultural and Allotment Association. Permanent allotment sites had already existed pre-war but more unused and recreational ground was changed to this use from 1940 on. Some parts of Haydon Hall, Field End Road, South Eastcote, the orchard opposite to Deane Parade shops, the site of the proposed new Methodist Church and the ground in front of St Andrew's Presbyterian Church were used for allotments. Whilst talking of food, one should not forget the invaluable service given by the British Restaurant which provided basic meals at low costs and operated from August 1942 to 1947 in the premises which now house the Post Office.

Other aspects of the war were similar to those in other parts of the country – gradual call up of males into the Armed Forces which in time extended to cover all males within the age range 18 to 42 unless judged to be in 'reserved' occupations. Then from 1941 there was compulsory registration of women for war work or service in the Forces. Those who did stay in the district during the war, were involved in other activities. These included firewatching duties at their place of work, first aid and other support services. Many joined the Womens Voluntary Service and others who were involved in Womens Institutes or organisations in churches found their activities directed towards support for the

70

Eastcote in Wartime

war effort in terms of bottling and food preservation, knitting comforts, correspondence with those away in the Forces or on war work and being involved temporarily in occupations which would normally have been filled by those called to other War service. Schools suffered from close down in the opening months of the War, depletion of staffs into the Forces – although this was to some extent overcome by allowing married women to come back into teaching – and physical deterioration of buildings either from war damage or non-maintenance. Normal school supplies were also at low level. Church attendances fell away as did the use and membership of many social organisations. However the Haydon Hall Cricket Club commenced in 1941 with members maintaining the ground in their spare time. Field End Club was formed in 1942 by a small band of ARP wardens.

Aerial attacks fell away after 1941 and did not recommence until 1944 when the V1 flying bomb and V2 rocket attacks began. Although none fell in the Eastcote district, residents were perpetually harrassed by foreboding and by the noise of these weapons passing overhead.

In April 1944 another use was found for Eastcote Place. As recorded by the late Godfrey Cornwall of the Rickmansworth Local History Society, Moor Park Mansion, just beyond Mount Vernon Hospital, became the HQ of 2nd Airborne Corps which was involved in the planning of Airborne activities over Europe from D Day to May 1945, including the venture at Arnhem. Eastcote Place became associated with this in housing a new Allied Troop Carrier Command Post. According to Lawrence Wright in his story of glider operations, Allied operations tended to remain separate and the Eastcote base acted mainly for telephonic coordination. Nevertheless he makes mention of Eastcote being in contact with General Browning's HQ at Nijmegen. However, his account of the house with its quilted gold bed-spreads, billiard room, swimming pool and hot house peaches explains why he describes it as being a pleasant place to hold parties for Airborne troops prior to their going into action. Also evocative is his memory of hearing an aircraft passing overhead with engine trouble and hoping it was an enemy craft; the cheering when it crashed and exploded followed by a later realisation that it had been a flying bomb.

EASTCOTE

POSTSCRIPT

By 1945 Eastcote had matured into an almost distinct community and had passed through a baptism of fire. From then until the present time changes have continued as one expects in any dynamic community. A continuing changeover in residents has occurred although a number of older village family descendants remain as do members of the 1920s and early 1930s incomers. Physical change has also taken place in landscape and buildings. Density of buildings, population and traffic has increased and it often happens that present day newcomers are unaware of the earlier formation of Eastcote. To anybody under the age of 45 the majority of buildings will be ten years and more older than they are. Eastcote was mainly laid out and saw major development during their parents' generation and when first seen today on emerging from the station, Eastcote appears to be an old established community.

Some of the significant changes which have taken place since the end of the Second World War will be mentioned here for the sake of completeness but not necessarily in chronological order. The station itself was found to be inadequate by the late 1930s and was redesigned in the then modern Charles Holden style as with many other LT stations of the period. It was virtually completed by the beginning of the war and was accompanied by a widening of the bridge. Due to post war restriction on public expenditure it was some years before the service road in front of the station was completed and during those years the space was firstly rather derelict and then improved by gardens. The Ideal Cinema and then Ideal Garages closed and were replaced by Initial House and the Health Authority offices. Although there were empty properties available in 1939 the houses were gradually filled during the course of the War following the movement of population out of London after the blitz. At the end of the War there was a great national shortage of housing and empty land and unfinished estates were rapidly developed. Some private housing was permitted under strict licence, but the main emphasis then was on building of houses by the local authority. Over 400 houses and flats were erected south of the railway with over 300 in the Fore Street and Wiltshire Lane area, including a small shopping centre in Salisbury Road. Orchard Parade shops were completed by the mid-1950s, with the branch library being opened by the Middlesex County Council in 1959.

The late 1940s and 1950s saw additional facilities and worries. The facilities were welcomed – Bourne School 1946; Field End Junior School in 1947 with an additional Infants School in 1952; Newnham Junior and Infants Schools in 1952; St Nicholas Grammar School 1955 and St Mary's Grammar School in 1957. The two latter have now been

How Eastcote Village had begun to expand by 1935.

combined to form Haydon School. The first part of the new Methodist Church in Pamela Gardens was completed by 1951 with the remainder of the Church building being consecrated in October 1960. The Cavendish Pavilion and Sports Ground was acquired for public use in February 1949 and the Pine Gardens Open Space in 1950. Residents had to become accustomed to a new form of street lighting during the early 1950s when the older gas lighting was replaced by electric sodium lighting. The main worry during this period was a spin-off from the Abercrombie Plan to relieve traffic congestion in Greater London. The part of the plan which would have materially changed the face of Eastcote was the infamous 'D' Ring Road. This bypass for through traffic would have run through the district, probably causing the demolition of the new Field End School and over 200 houses. It would have passed through the Eastcote Recreation Ground and over Eastcote village and Haydon Hall on a stilted overpass. This threat was not finally removed until 1957.

1949 had also seen the purchase by the local authority of High Grove and its remaining grounds. Part of the grounds were set aside for a new Civic Centre for the RNUDC which was coupled with the petition by the Council for granting of Borough status. This was rejected in 1956 and the plans for new offices were not proceeded with. Part of the grounds, however, were used for the Highgrove Bath which was opened in July, 1964. Just after the end of the Second World War the Eastcote Community Association was formed with a new Community Hall in Southbourne Gardens. In the 1960s both Eastcote House and Haydon Hall were demolished although their grounds were retained for public use. 1964 saw the demolition of The Barns for the creation of Farthings Close and Eastcote Lodge for the building of Flag Walk. These were closely followed by the acquisition of Eastcote Place and grounds for the development of Georgian Court and Azalea Walk. Farthings Close, Azalea Walk and Flag Walk were developed by Prowtings of Ruislip. Fortunately, Eastcote Place was retained and converted into flats. Eastcote did not altogether escape the building of commercial premises during the 1960s and 1970s and these lie immediately to the south of the railway.

The closing of the smithy and the erection of a 'modern' shopping parade would seem to have finalised the transition of a village to a suburb. Under the Civic Amenities Act 1967, the London Borough of Hillingdon, which had superseded the RNUDC in 1965, created fifteen Conservation Areas. One of these was to cover Eastcote Village and the open spaces of Haydon Hall, Eastcote House and Long Meadow between the High Road and the River Pinn. Perhaps the village has now risen as a phoenix to have a new lease of life within the suburb.

ACKNOWLEDGEMENTS

Hillingdon Library Service, especially Brian Williams for his oversight of the text and many helpful suggestions and to Carolynne Cotton for source material and Jane Wood for preparation of index.
Bob Thompson, Local History Section, Harrow Library Service
Eastcote Womens Institute
Mr Trowbridge, Farr Bedford & Co
Mrs Sefton, Eastcote Chamber of Commerce
Iris Long, Research Group, Pinner Local History Society
Tony and Angela Vincent
Fred and Connie Older
Mr A. C. V. Telling
Jack and Toni Page
Mrs E. W. Crane
Alan A. Jackson
Many residents of Eastcote
London Transport Museum
Middlesex County Press

SOURCES

Victoria County History
W. A. G. Kemp: "The History of Eastcote"
"The Church Monthly" and St Martin's Church, Ruislip Parish Magazine 1890-1901
"The Ideal Home" August 1925
"Homes and Gardens" November 1934
"The Middlesex & Buckinghamshire Advertiser"
"Advertiser and Gazette"
T. F. Nash Ltd publicity material
"The Aerial" published by Eastcote Association
"Metro-Land"
Kelly's directories
D. Massey: "Ruislip-Northwood: The Development of the Suburb with special reference to the period 1887-1914"
Research material of the late David Tottman and the late W. A. G. Kemp
Annual Medical Reports RNUDC 1905-17
RNUDC Minutes December 1911-July 1913
Alan A. Jackson: "Semi-Detached London"
"The Battle of Britain Then and Now" Ed W. G. Ramsey
"Action Stations 8" B. B. Halpenny
"Flying High" Air Vice Marshal S. F. Vincent
"The Wooden Sword" Lawrence Wright
Jubilee and Anniversary booklets of St Lawrence and Eastcote Methodist churches
"Bulletin" of St Andrew's United Reform Church
RNUDC Jubilee booklets

INDEX

Page numbers in **bold type** refer to illustrations

Abbotsbury Gardens 37, 46
Abercrombie Mr and Mrs 17
Acacia Avenue 25, 34
Addison, Dr Christopher 32
Agnew, Thomas and Sons 56
agriculture 12, 22, 32: animals 14: arable farming 14: farms 13: hay 14: pigs 42
air raids 61-**63**, 65-66, 69, **71**: precautions 64
allotments 70
almshouses 19
Anderson, Sir John 31
Anderson, Lady 31
Anglicans 53, 65
Appleton, E. H. 27
Aragon Drive 43
Ascott Court 13
athletics 31
Azalea Walk 74

Bailey, A. 21
Baker, L. Ingham 17
Ball, George 43
Barns, The 13, 31, 69, 74
Bayetto, Capt. T. H. 61
Bayly, Arthur B. 31
Beaulieu Drive 57
Beech Avenue 25-26
Bennett Edwards see Edwards Bennett
Benson's Hall see Old Barn
Bessingby Recreation Ground 59
Bishop Winnington-Ingram C. of E. School 57
'Black Horse' Inn 57
Boer War 61
'Bogs' The 42
Boldmere Road 42
Boundary Road 42
Bourne, Cardinal 31
Bourne Farm 13
Bourne School 73
Bovis Homes 42
bowls 35, 56
Boyle, John 11
Bridle Road 9, 25-27, 31, 36, 41-42, 53-54, 69
Bright, Jeremiah 16
British Freehold Investments Syndicate 25-26, 35-36, 44
British Restaurant 70
Broadhurst Gardens 43
Brooklands see Hornend
Burwood Avenue 37
buses 34, 49, 67
butchers 32
Button, Alfred and Son, grocery firm 32

Campbell, Sir Hugh Hume 12
Campbell, Lady Hume 16
Cannonbury Avenue 42, 57
Cannon Lane 57
Cannon Lane Primary School 46, 57
Cardinal Road 43
Carew, Frances Murray 22
Carter, Miss 13
Carter, C. J. 56
'Case is Altered' Inn 57
Castleton Road 43
Catlins Lane 9, 22, 31, 55, 65
Cavendish Amateur Athletics Association 31: Pavilion and Sports Ground 56, 74
cemetery 51
Chamberlain, Neville 65
Chandos Road 42
Chapel Hill 9, 13, 22, 36-37, 51, 53
Chapel of the Blessed Thomas More 53
charities 46: Bright's 16: Campbell's 16
Chase, The 37, 41-42, 69
Chelston Road 44
Cheney Farm 13, 44-45
Cheney Hill Estate 26
Cheney Street 9, 13, 22, **26**-27, 31, 36, 52-54
Churches see Chapel of the Blessed Thomas More, Methodist Chapel, Mission Church, St. Andrew's Presbyterian C. of E. Church, St. Lawrence's Church, St. Martin's Church, Ruislip, St. Thomas More R.C. Church, Most Sacred Heart R.C. Church, Ruislip, see also religious denominations
Churchill, Lady Randolph 12
Churchill, Winston 12, 68-69
Churton, Miss 28
Cinema: Ideal 35, 46, 55, 66-67, 73
Circuits, The 13
Clapham Park 31
Clarke, Adam 53
clay pigeon shooting 42
Clements, Miss 34
Cleves Way 43
Close, The 69
Colne, River 10
Colne Valley Water Company 22
Comben and Wakeling 36-37, 41-42, 54
Commerce, Chamber of 46
Community Hall 34, 55 see also Ideal Cinema
Coniston Gardens 44
conservation areas 74
Corn Laws: repeal of 14
Cornwall, Godfrey 71
Coronation: George VI, celebrations 46
Coteford Close 29, 32, 34
Coteford Junior and Infants School 46

76

Crack, David 12
Crane, Mrs 53
Crescent Gardens 37, 41
cricket 51, 55: Field End Cricket Club 71: Haydon Hall Cricket Club 71
Crouch, G. T. Ltd 43
Cuckoo Hill 9, 13, 22, 27, 36
Cuckoo Hill Farm 13
cycling 31, 49, 58

Davis Estates Ltd 43-44
Deane Croft Road 37, **41**-42, 45, 69
Deane Estate 36, 42
Deane Parade 45, 47, 67, 70
Deane R. Hawtrey 11, 36-37, 53
Deane Way 37
Decontamination Centre 64, **66**
Devon Parade 45, 64
Devonshire Lodge 36, 46
Devonshire Road 37, 69
diet 19-20
disease 15, 24, 62
District Railway **1**, 40, 42 see also Piccadilly Line
drainage 9, 11, 23-24, 26, 32, 42, 62
Dyer, Margaret Ward 52
Dyer, Mrs Ward 32

Ealing 19, 57
Eastbury Estate 22
Eastcote Allotment Association 70: Bowling Club 56: bypass 74: Camera Club 59: Chess Club 59: Choral Society 59: Community Association 74: Community Hall 34, 55: Coronation Players 59: Cottage 22: Country Club 55: Cricket Team 51, 55: Decontamination Centres 64, **66:** End Park Estate **30**, 34-35, 55: Fencing Club 59: Football Team 51, 55: Garden Estate 44: Guides 58: Halt 22, 25: House 11, 14, 31, 36-37, 54, 59, 68, 74: Keep Fit Classes 59: Lawn Tennis Club 55, 56: Library 73: Lodge 13, 17, 61, 74: Mother's Outing 17: Old Persons Tea 17: Park Estate 36-37,42, 44, **45**, 69: Place 11, 31, 69, 71, 74: Players 59: Point 13: Pumping Station 22: Rambling Club 59: Recreation Ground 56, 74: Refugee Committee 65: Residents' Associations 34, 52, 56, 59, 64: Road 17, 22, 51, 57, 69: Scouts 58: Slate Club 17: Smithy 9, **12**, 59, 74: Station 31, **33**, 35, **48, 49,** 58, 61, 64, 66, 73: Village **8, 72,** 74: Village Institute 17, 51-54, 57, 59: War Memorial **60**-62: Women's Institute 52, 54, 59
Eastern Avenue 42
Eden, Anthony 68
education see schools
Edwards, Capt Bennett 11
Edwards, Mrs Bennett 11, 19, 31
Edwards, Mrs George 28
'Eight Bells' Inn 49
elections 32
electricity 32, 35, 37-38, 42
Elm Avenue 25, 27, 46
Elm Grove see Elm Avenue

employment 12, 16, 17, 23: income 38
Essex Close 43
'Eventide Homes' 39
Everett Close 34
Everitt, H. 27

Fairway, The 14
farming see agriculture
Farthings Close 13, 74
Ferncroft Avenue 43
Field Close see Maple Close
Field End 22
Field End Cricket Club 71
Field End Farm 13, 36
Field End House 13, 31, 53-54
Field End Junior and Infants School 73-74
Field End Lodge 31, 61
Field End·Parade 34, 45-46, 55, 67
Field End Road 9, 13, 22, 27, 31, 34, 36, 41, 43, 45-46, 52-54, 69-70
Field End Villas 13, 31
Flag Cottage 13, 19
Flag Walk 13, 74
Food Control Office 68
football 51, 55
footpaths 9-10, 37
Fore Street 9, 13, 22, 28-29, 34, 44, 46, 52-53, 55, 57, 59, 73
Fore Street Farm 13, 44
Forresters, The 42
Forsyth, W. A. 53
Four Elms Farm 9, 13
Frewin, Noel 46
Frog Lane see Fore Street
Fuller, Juliana Rebecca 12
Furness, Sir Christopher M.P. 21
'Fyvie' 52

Galley, C. V. 42, 44
Gallop, Henry 12
Garth Close 43
gas lighting 74
gas supply 32, 35, 37-38, 42
George VI, King 69: Coronation celebrations 46
Georgian Court 74
Gerrard Gardens 44
Gillett, Mr 47
Girl's Friendly Society 52
Glen, The 37
Golding, Mr 32
golf 11
Godwin, Rev. R. F. 53
Goschen, Kenneth 31, 50, 53
Grail Community 53
Grange, The 13, 44
Greencroft Avenue 43
Greenhill 22
Guides 58

Hall, B. J. 61
Harrow 9, 19, 31, 42, 55, 57: station 21-22
Harrow Weald Common 10
Hartley, E. S. 55

77

Haste Hill 10, 58
Hatch End 9
Hawthorn Avenue 25, 34, 37, **38-39**
Hawthornden Prize for Literature 11
Hawtrey family 11, 37
Hawtrey, R. Deane see Deane R. Hawtrey
Haydon Hall 11, **16,** 19, 31, 53, 59, 64-65, 69-70, 74: Cricket Club 71: Decontamination Centre 64, **66:** stables 9
Haydon Hall Farm 13
Haydon Lodge 19
Haydon School 73
Hayes 23
High Grove 11-12, 19, 31, 51, 53, 56, 74
Highgrove Bath 74
High Meadow 65
High Road 9, 13-14, 17, 36, 44, 61
Hignett, Dr. 9-10, 62
Hillingdon Health Authority 73
Hillingdon, London Borough of 74
Hinman, Mrs 53
Hinman family 52 see also Dyer, Mrs Ward
Holder's field 44
Home Guard 68
Hornend 13, 31, 52, 54
hospitals 61: St. Vincent's Cripples Home and School for Defective Children 31-32, 46-47, 69
housing 9, 11, 13, 15, 22, 24-32, 34-38, 40-46, 59, 73: prices 19, 41, 44
Hume-Campbell Sir Hugh see Campbell, Sir Hugh Hume

Ickenham 9, 42
Ideal Cinema 35, 46, 55, 66-67, 73
Ideal Garages 73
Ideal Motors 57
Imperial Estate 26
industry 70
Ingram Rt. Rev. A. F. Winnington 53
Initial House 73
inns 9: 'Black Horse' 57: 'Case is Altered' 57: 'Eastcote Arms' 10: 'Eight Bells' 49, 51: 'Manor House' 57: 'Ship' 13, **18,** 22, 57: 'Woodman' 57
Institute see Village Institute
Ivy Close 42
Ivy Farm 13, 32

Joel Street 9, 13, 22, 31, 34, 36, 44, 55, 59
Joel Street Farm 13

Kerswell, H. H. 70
Kings' College 22, 24, 25

Lavender family 32
Lavender, Eva 32, 58
lawn tennis 35, 55-56
Lawrence, Mrs 53
Lee, Mr 55
libraries: private 46: public 46, 73
lighting: domestic 32: street 37, 51, 65, 74: war time regulations 65, 67
Lime Grove 25, 27, 56

Linden Avenue 25-26, 44
local government: London Borough of Hillingdon 74: Middlesex County Council 24, 57, 73: Overseers of the Poor 9: Ruislip-Northwood Urban District Council 9, 24-27, 29, 34, 37, 42, 54, 56, 62, 64, 69, 74: Ruislip Parish Council 9, 23: Uxbridge Rural District Council 9, 21, 23: Vestry 23
Local Government Board 23, 25
London and North Western Railway 9
London, Bishop of 53
London General Omnibus Company 49
London Passenger Transport Board 49
London Transport 66-67, 73
Long Meadow 74
Lowlands Road 37, 41, 55

Manor Homes 44
Manor Homes Estates 43
'Manor House Inn' 57, 62
Manor Secondary School 57
Manor Way 29, 51
Maple Close 37, 41
Meadow Way 37, **40-**41
Methodist Chapel 9, 51, **53,** 64, 67, 70, 74
Methodist London Mission and Extension Fund 54
Methodists 53, 58, 64-65, 67
Metropolitan Railway 9, 21-24, 32, 40, 42, 47, 61, 66-67: Eastcote Halt 22, 25: Eastcote Station 31, **33,** 35, **48, 49,** 58, 61, 64, 66, 73: fares 40: Harrow Station 22: Northwood Station 22: Northwood Hills Station 34: Pinner Station 9: Rayners Lane Station 47, 49, 67: Ruislip Manor Station 43: Ruislip Station 22: travelling conditions 47, 67
Middlesex County Council 24, 57, 73
milk 14-15, 32
Millar, C. W. 31
Miss Carter's Private School 13, 19
Mission Church 53
Missouri Court 41-42
Mistletoe Farm 13, 31
Moor Park Mansion 71
Morford Close 34
Morford Way 34-**35,** 55
mortality statistics 15, 24, 62
Most Sacred Heart R.C. Church, Ruislip 54
motor traffic 31-32, 40
Mount Park Estate 36, 44
Mount Park Road 44
Murch, W. J. 31
Myer, Bishop 59
Myrtle Avenue 25, 34, 56
Myrtle Farm 13, 32

Napoleonic Wars 61
Nash family 41
Nash, S. G. 42
Nash, T. F. 36-38, 41-42, 45-46, 69
Nash, T. F. (Investment) Ltd 54
National Schools see Schools
New House see Eastcote Place

New Model Farm 13
Newnham Junior and Infants School 73
Nicholson, Sir Charles 53
Norfolk, Duke of 31
Northolt Aerodrome 61, 68-69
Northolt Junction 25
Northolt Road 9, 13, 27, 31, 43
North View 42, 46
Northwood 14, 22-24, 29, 32, 49, 51, 65: Council School 15, 19, 51, 57: Electric Company 32: Golf Club 11: Station 22
Northwood Hills Station 34

Oak Grove 25-26, 44
Old Barn 22, 28
Old Barn House 13
Orchard Parade 62, 70, 73
Overseer of the Poor 17

Page, J. P. Estate 26
Pamela Gardens 37, 53-54, 64, 74
Pavilion: entertainment grounds 31, 36, 42, 43
Pavilion Way 44
Peel, Arthur 12
Peel, Sir Robert 12
petition 39
Philip family 52, 54
Philip, Mrs 53
Philip, George 52, 59
Piccadilly Line 40, 67
Pine Gardens 44, 69
Pine Gardens Open Space 74
Pinn, River 10, 37, 42, 74
Pinner 9, 13, 19, 49: County School 19, 51, 57: Gas Works 32: Hill 10: National School 19, 51: Station 9
police 67
poor relief 17, 19
population 9, 11, 14, 16, 32, 47, 55
post office 13, 32, 62, 70
poverty 11-12, 15-17, 23, 27, 29
Presbyterians 54, 59, 64
Presbytery: North London Church Extension Committee 54
Prowtings 74
public health 62: animal hygiene 14-15, Colne Valley Water Company 22: disease 15, 24, 62: drainage 9-11, 23-24, 26, 32, 42, 62: housing 27: refuse 22: sewers 9, 22, 26, 29: tuberculin testing of milk 15: water supply 9, 14, 22, 24, 26, 32, 35, 42
public houses see inns
pumping station 22

Queen's Parade 46

railways see Metropolitan Railway, District Railway, Piccadilly Line
Ratcliffe, Mrs 32
rationing 68, 70
Rayners Lane 42: station 47, 49, 67
'Red Lion' Inn 49
refugees 63, 65

refuse 22
Retreat Cottage 13
Retreat, The 31
Ritchie, Dr. R. 62
rivers see Pinn River, Colne River
roads 9-11, 23, 25, 32, 37-38, 44-45, 51, 73-74; petition **39**
Rodney Gardens 37, 42
Roman Catholics 9, 53, 54
Rosery, The 22
Rotherham Estates Ltd 36-37, **40**-42, 45
Rowntree, Seebohm 16
'Royal Highlander' 49
Rushdene Road 37, 42, 54
Ruislip 9, 14-15, 19, 22-24, 28-29: Holt 31: House 31: National Schools 15, 17, 19, 24, 51, 57: Northwood Urban District Council 9, 24-27, 29, 34, 37, 42, 54, 56, 62, 64, 69, 74: Northwood Workmen's Housing Council 29: Parish Council 9, 23: Reservoir 58: Station 22: Woods 58
Ruislip Manor 42-44, 59, 69: Cottage Society 28-29, 34, 55: Station 43

St. Andrew's Presbyterian C. of E. Church 54, 64, 67, 69, 70
St. Lawrence's Church 53, **56,** 62, 67: church hall 53, 62
St. Lawrence Drive 37, 41, 42, 59, 67
St. Martin's Church, Ruislip 9, 51, 53, 61
St. Mary's Grammar School 73
St. Nicholas's Grammar School 73
St. Thomas More R.C. Church 13, 54
St. Vincent's Cripples Home and School for Defective Children 31-32, 46-47, 69
Sainsbury, J. Ltd 46
Salisbury Road 73
schools 19, 51, 57, 58, 71: Bishop Winnington Ingram C. of E. School 57: Bourne School 73: Cannon Lane Primary School 46, 57: Coteford Junior School 46: Field End Junior and Infants School 73-74: Haydon School 73: Manor Secondary School 57: Miss Carter's Private School 13, 19: Newnham Junior and Infants School 73: Northwood Council School 15, 19, 51: Pinner County School 19, 51, 57: Pinner National School 19, 51: Ruislip National Schools 15, 17, 19, 24, 51, 57: St. Mary's Grammar School 73: St. Nicholas's Grammar School 73: St. Vincent's Cripples Home and School for Defective Children 31-32, 46-47, 69: Uxbridge County School 57 see also Sunday Schools
Scouts 58-59
sewers 9, 22, 26, 29
Seymour Gardens 43
'Ship' Inn 9, 13, **18**, 22, 57
shops 32, 34, 45-46, 52, 62, 67, 70, 74
'Sigers' 13, 31, 42, 50, 53
Sigers, The 31
Smith Brothers 44
smithy 9, **12,** 59, 74
social life 17, 19, 22, 31, 42, 46, 51-53, 55-56, 58-59, 65-67, 71
soil 9-10, 26

79

Soutar Messrs. A. & F. 29
South Eastcote 69-70
Southbourne Gardens 44, 74
Southill Farm 13
Southill House 17, 61
Southill Lane 9, 13
Spencer Estate 44
Spencer, W. Ltd. 44
sport: athletics 31; bowls 35,, 56: clay pigeon shooting 42: cricket 51, 55, 71: fencing 59: football 51, 55: golf 11: lawn tennis 35, 55-56: swimming 74
Spring Cottage see Flag Cottage
Stanmore 68
Station Approach 46, 64
Sullivan, Capt 11
Sunday Schools 54, 58
'Sunnyside' 31, 55
supermarkets: J. Sainsbury Ltd. 46: Watford Co-operative Society 46: Tesco Stores Ltd 46
Sutton Close 44
Sweden, Dowager Queen of 12
swimming 74

Taylor Woodrow 43
Telcote Parade 46
telephone 32
television 47
Telling, A. C. V. 34
Telling Brothers Ltd **30**, 34-36, 45, 55
Telling, W. A. T. Ltd 34
Tesco Stores Ltd 46
Thompson, Alderman 29
transport: buses 34, 49, 67: District Railway **1,** 40, 42: horse drawn traffic 9: Metropolitan Railway 9, 21-22, 24, 32, 40, 42, 47, 61, 66-67: motor traffic 31-32, 40: Piccadilly Line 40, 67
trees 25, 41
Tudor Close 44
Tudor Estate 44

Underground Railway see District Railway, Metropolitan Railway, Piccadilly Line
Uxbridge 19, 21, 24, 31, 57: bus garage 49: County School 57: Rural District Council 9, 21, 23: Station 21, 67: War time operations room 68

Vestry 23
Victoria Road 44
Village Institute 17, 51-53, 55, 57, 59

Vincent Gp Capt S. F. 68
Vincent Estates 43
Vivian, Mrs 53

wages 38
Walker, Rev. Dr. Thomas 54
walking 31-32, 49, 59
Ward, Mrs Dyer see Dyer, Mrs Ward
War Memorial 13, **60**, 61-62
Warrender, Alice 11, 31
Warrender, Eleanor 11, 19, 31, 53, 56
Warrender, Vice Admiral Sir George 12
Warrender Park 56
water supply 9, 14, 22, 24, 26, 32, 35, 42
Watford 19, 32: Co-operative Society 46
Wealdstone 23
Webb, Maurice 50
Wembley 57
Wentworth Drive 44
W. G. Estates Ltd 43
Whitby Road 44
White, A. G. 42
White, A. G. Developments Ltd 54
Wiltshire Lane 9, 13, 22, 26, 32, 34, 73
Winnington-Ingram see Ingram Rt. Rev. A. F. Winnington
Winslow Close 41-42
Winter, Miss 53
Women's Industrial Council 28
Women's Institute: Eastcote 52-54: Field End 59: South Ruislip 59: support for war effort 70-71
Women's Voluntary Service 70
Woodlands Avenue 31, 42, 44, 67
Woodlands Avenue Estate 26
'Woodman' Inn 57
World War I: 29, 32, 34-35, 37, 53: air raids 61-62: prisoners of war 61: war memorial 13, **60**, 62: wounded 61
World War II: 34, 55, 62, 64: air raid precautions 64, 67: Allied Troop Carrier Command Post 69: British Restaurant 70: Dig for Victory Campaign 70: Food Control Office 68: Home Guard 68: rationing 68, 70
Wright, Mr. 9
Wright, Lawrence 71
Wylchin Close 34

Yeading Brook 69
Yiewsley 10